SQUARE WORDS
IN A ROUND WORLD

Eric Waldram Kemp was born near Grimsby, Lincolnshire, and educated at Brigg Grammar School, Exeter College, Oxford and St Stephen's House, Oxford. Ordained in 1939 he was Librarian of Pusey House, Oxford 1941–6, and later became Fellow, Chaplain, Tutor and Lecturer in Theology and Medieval History at Exeter College. From 1952 to 1969 he was the Bishop of Oxford's Commissary for Religious Communities, and in 1960 was named Honorary Provincial Canon of Capetown. He became Bishop of Chichester in 1974.

Dr Kemp has contributed to many books and journals, and amongst his own writings is *The Life and Letters of Kenneth Escott Kirk, 1937–54*, the biography of his father-in-law, the former Bishop of Oxford.

SQUARE WORDS
IN A
ROUND WORLD

Eric Waldram Kemp, D.D.
Bishop of Chichester

*With a Foreword by
the Archbishop of Canterbury,
Dr Donald Coggan*

With best wishes,

+ Eric Cicestr:

9 May 1980

Collins
FOUNT PAPERBACKS
in association with Faith Press

First published by Fount Paperbacks
in association with Faith Press in 1980

© Eric Waldram Kemp 1980

Made and printed in Great Britain by
William Collins Sons & Co Ltd, Glasgow

For
Sarah, Katharine, Alice, Harriet
and Edward

CONTENTS

FOREWORD

A very great many people today want to know what the Christian faith is all about – is it possible for an intelligent person to be a believer? Does Christianity provide a way of thinking and acting which is deserving of serious consideration or even of someone's total loyalty?

These are serious questions, and they are being asked by many seriously-minded people.

The Bishop of Chichester has for the major part of his ministry been a university teacher. He has the skill which enables him, against a background of wide reading and clear thinking, to set out, clearly and without too technical language, what the Christian faith is about. This he does for us in this Lent Book for 1980.

I am grateful to him for what he has written and for the way he has written it. I hope the book will be widely read and will bring light and understanding to many.

Lambeth Palace,   DONALD CANTUAR:
London, SE1.

INTRODUCTION

In writing this book I have tried to present the Christian faith and life as a coherent whole, for I believe it is that coherence which, more than the argument for any bit of it, convinces one of its truth. For that reason I would recommend those who wish to use it for Lent reading to read straight through it in as short a time as they can, and then to take it chapter by chapter through the weeks of Lent. I think that it will be found more helpful in this way.

The title was suggested to me some years ago by my friend Eric Turnbull, when I was giving a course of Lent talks at Worcester where he is a canon and I was dean. I was grateful to him for it then, and I have retained it for this much re-written and expanded version of those talks because it expresses the important truth that Christianity can be an uncomfortable religion. In the second chapter I have expressed reservations about modes of conduct which are defended because they are 'natural'. St Paul tells us that we are not to be conformed to this world but to be transformed by the renewing of our minds – in other words, if we want to be true followers of Christ we must be prepared for a change of outlook. That is what the title is intended to suggest.

Little of what I have written is original, and I am grateful to my teachers at University and Theological College and to many others from whom I have learned and continue to learn. I am grateful to my secretary, Miss Mary Balmer, for typing and re-typing the book, and to my chaplain, the Rev. Keith Hobbs, and his wife for checking the text.

✝ERIC CICESTR:

Chichester, July 1979

I. CREATION

There was a small boy who lived with his mother in a house in the country. On one summer evening he was sent to bed earlier than usual because his mother was having an evening party and wanted him out of the way. In bed he listened to the sounds of people arriving, heard them in the garden below his window, and got out of bed to go and watch. As he looked out of the window and saw his mother moving about among her guests, talking and laughing with them, it came to him with a sense of shock that she had a life of her own, a life independent of him.

I suspect that that incident is similar to the experience of most of us. As we grow up we become increasingly aware of the world around us as independent of ourselves, even hostile in a way, and one of the first and most fundamental acts of faith that we make is in this independence of others and of the universe. We accept that it is not all just in our imagination, in our mind, but has a reality of its own. I don't think that anyone can ever prove this in a conclusive, mathematical sort of way, not even by kicking the table with one's bare feet and finding that it hurts, but this act of faith in the reality and independence of the universe is something that we find essential to living – a necessary hypothesis.

Let us look at another kind of act of faith – one that we make in our relationships with other people. The characters in a play or a novel are not real people, and therefore it is possible to know all that there is to know about them. There is no point in asking how Mr Pickwick or Oliver Twist would behave in such and such circumstances, because the answer is that they would behave as Charles Dickens, if he were alive, would decide that they should.

In other words we are referred behind the fictional characters to the author, himself a real person, and what uncertainty there is lies in him, not in them. However well we think that we know a real person we can never be quite sure what he will say or do, how he will react to some test or crisis. But in life it is necessary that we put our trust in others. We do this in many ways all day long. The majority of us do it in a most complete way when we embark upon marriage. We use such evidence as is available to us from observation, from experience. We use our reason upon the evidence so that our choice may be a rational choice, but in the end the choice, the decision, has to be made, and is an act of faith.

Let us look at something else which arises from our own experience, namely how we try to get at the truth about things, how we try to understand the reality of the world and the situations in which we live. Reflecting on this we may be surprised to find how large a place is occupied by stories and by symbols of one kind or another, by fiction and by poetry. For many people it is much easier to get into the heart of the past, to feel that one has an understanding of other ages and states of society, through a historical novel, rather than through a straight history book – through a piece of imaginative writing, rather than through a narrative of facts. The cult, it is not too strong a word, of the writings of Professor Tolkien is a demonstration of the power of imaginative literature to express significant truth. I would hazard a guess also that insights into the truth are conveyed to far more people by fiction, poetic or prose, than by philosophy.

When we think about Creation, the first of our square words, we are almost inevitably directed to the great classic story of the creation of the world in the Book of Genesis. The whole Christian religion rests on the principles expressed in that story, but before we look at them let us think how this story of Creation relates to the three aspects of human experience which I have just described.

First, it is a story of a symbolic kind. Few people nowadays would dream of treating it as a scientific account of the stages by which the universe came into being, and it is doubtful whether people ever so regarded it for more than a few of the many centuries that the story has been in existence. It is, like most of the first eleven chapters of Genesis, the Hebrew form of certain common beliefs concerning the beginning of the earth and of man which prevailed in the circle of nations to which both Babylonians and Hebrews belonged. It is, however, worthy of our attention because of what distinguishes it from the other ancient or more ancient forms of those beliefs, for the Genesis story is a refinement of the Babylonian ones, showing a deeper spiritual reflection and insight.

The Babylonian stories are tales and little more. They are like the legends embodied in the Norse sagas or the old Greek legends. They are polytheistic. A primeval watery chaos (Tiamat) antedates the deities, who gradually came into being singly or in pairs. Eventually the gods appoint Marduk as their champion in a great fight with Tiamat, who is defeated and cut in two to form the firmament above the organized world and the abyss of waters supporting it below. Marduk gains his supremacy only after a long contest and then, rather as an afterthought, creates man 'that the service of the gods may be established and that their shrines may be built'. The Genesis version is sufficiently close in some matters of detail to indicate a common origin, but comparison shows that the common source is being altered and used to give expression to certain beliefs.

These are, like the first two kinds of human experience with which we started, assertions of faith in the nature of the universe and in a person – the Creator of it. The reason why I began this chapter by talking about those kinds of experience was to prepare for the right approach to the Biblical account of Creation – that is, to see it as an expression of belief couched in the form of a story, a belief involving commitment of a personal kind and action or behaviour appropriate to that commitment. Of course none of that guarantees its truth, but then I am not setting out to prove its truth. It is not my purpose here to try to prove the existence of God, even if I could. What I shall try to do is to show the Christian faith as a coherent and reasonable whole, and to have that picture of it is a very important part of being a Christian.

'In the beginning God created the heavens and the earth.' By contrast with those other and older stories we have here one god only, one source of creation only. Everything that is has been made by God and depends upon him at all time. Six hundred years ago an English woman saw it like this:

And he showed me more, a little thing, the size of a hazel-nut, on the palm of my hand, round like a ball. I looked at it thoughtfully and wondered, 'What is this?' And the answer came, 'It is all that is made.' I marvelled that it continued to exist and did not suddenly disintegrate; it was so small. And again my mind supplied the answer, 'It exists, both now and for ever, because God loves it.' In short, everything owes its existence to the love of God.

In this 'little thing' I saw three truths. The first is that God made it; the second is that God loves it; and the third is that God sustains it.[1]

Part of the Christian belief is that everything is sustained in being by God, and if it were not so sustained would cease to be, would vanish into nothingness. In other words, God is not like a motor-car manufacturer whose factory makes a car, sells it, and then has no more responsibility for it, nor even like the man who makes a washing machine and offers a service contract with it. God is involved in the continued being of what he has made, and so long as we exist we can never be separated from him. The words of Psalm 139 try to express this:

If I climb up into heaven thou art there: if I go down to hell thou art there also. If I take the wings of the morning: and remain in the uttermost parts of the sea; Even there also shall thy hand lead me: and thy right hand shall hold me.

This is the foundation of Christian spirituality, as that quotation from Julian of Norwich, coming so near the beginning of her book *Revelations of Divine Love*, shows.

People have followed this out in three ways. One has been to look at the grandeur and the beauty of the universe, whether it be the starry sky or the mountain tops, or the vastness of the sea, the beauty of sunset, the varied green of the countryside in spring, or the marvellous colours of a butterfly or a humming-bird – to look at these things and to say in the words of the children's hymn:

> All things bright and beautiful
> All creatures great and small
> All things wise and wonderful
> The Lord God made them all.

This is to see the Creator in the Creation and to catch a glimpse of the immensity, the majesty, the beauty of God.

A second way has been to look at life around us and to see in human love, in courage, in nobility of character, in humility and in patience, reflections of the divine nature, and to be moved, uplifted, strengthened by what we see. And this looking at life around us need not be confined to that which goes on now. It can take in all human history, so that by dwelling on the past, whether in the Bible or in the stories of noble and good lives in other

17

ages, we are inspired to face the present rather than escape
from it. St Paul has something to say about this:

> Fill your minds with everything that is true, everything
> that is noble, everything that is good and pure, every-
> thing that we love and honour, and everything that can
> be thought virtuous or worthy of praise . . . Then the
> God of peace will be with you. (Philippians 4:8–9)

The third way is to look within oneself, to find God in the
depths of one's own being, as when a man is quiet and
still, trying to concentrate wholly upon God, conscious of
his sustaining hands. This is for many people the heart
of prayer, and I will say no more about it now for we
must return to this theme in another chapter. What we
may observe, however, before we pass on to another point,
is that these three ways, or approaches to our Creator and
sustainer, are indications of three distinct relationships
with him which have their place in the experiences which
have led men to speak of the Trinity in Unity. And that
too is a subject to which we must later return.

Now we pass on from the Bible's distinctive assertion of
the one unique Creator and sustainer of all things, to an
equally emphatic assertion about the nature of all that he
has made. The six days of Creation in the Genesis story
present a series of representative pictures of the various
stages by which the earth was gradually formed, and
peopled with its living inhabitants. The story insists on
the unity of their first cause, God himself. It does not
profess to say anything about the secondary causes, the
details, which it is the province of the various branches
of natural science to investigate. But the story insists on
something else which can be seen to follow from the unity
of the first cause, namely that everything that God has
made is good. The ancient Hebrews were as well aware as
we are of evil-doing, of disease, of natural disasters, but
their own reflection, their spiritual insight, led them right

away from certain theories about those things which have always attracted some minds, and they asserted the essential goodness of the whole created universe. Through the story of the days runs the refrain 'God saw that it was good', and at the end 'God saw all that he had made, and indeed it was very good.' We do not perhaps realize the full significance of this because its opposing religion, dualism, is not so consciously and forcibly presented in our day as in some former ages. Nevertheless dualism is often unconsciously assumed and lies behind some of the deviations from Christianity. By dualism in this context is generally meant an approach to the problem of evil which posits two opposing sources of being, one the origin of spirit and the other the origin of matter. Spirit tends to be identified with what is good, and matter with what is evil, and in practice this kind of dualism has curiously led to two very different patterns of conduct. On the one hand some have said: 'If the body, being matter, is evil it must be mortified, denied, subdued in every conceivable way.' And so extreme asceticism is adopted to free the spirit from the body, the logical conclusion of which should be suicide. But some others have said: 'If the body, being matter, is evil then it cannot be of any significance what we do with it. Let us therefore indulge it to the full.' And so we get extreme licentiousness, the casting aside of all moral restraint.

By contrast the Bible asserts that matter and spirit are not to be opposed to one another in this way, that both come from the one Creator and both are good. And in reference to our human nature this means that we must not make a sharp division between spirit and matter, exalting what we call the spiritual as having more to do with God, and depressing the material as having less to do with God. Modern medicine has produced an ugly but important word, 'psychosomatic', which is intended to express the deep involvement of spirit and matter with each other, the impossibility in this life of separating body and

19

soul. The distinction that the Christian makes is not between those who are dominated by the body and those who are dominated by the spirit, for we are all of us a unity, but between those whose outlook is limited by this world and this life, and those who have the larger dimension of a knowledge of the Creator and of a life beyond this life. This is the contrast meant by St Paul when he writes, as so often he does, of those who are earthly and those who are spiritual. Within orthodox Christianity there are two types of practice which at first sight might seem to resemble the two extremes which result from dualism. There are those who are sometimes called world-renouncing and those sometimes called world-affirming. But these are misleading terms because both affirm the goodness of Creation although they believe themselves called to different attitudes towards it. For one group there is the call to find God in his creatures, in what he has made. For the other there is the call to find God by renunciation of some of his creatures. Both groups see themselves called to serve God but in different ways, as the members of one body have different functions. So within the Christian community there are the monks and nuns, and other ascetics, whose call to the service of God and of their brethren requires the abandonment of certain pleasures, certain ties, certain relationships, certain freedoms, and there are the many others whose service is through the right use of the very things which the others have renounced. The two are complementary in the Christian family, both affirming – but in different ways – the Creator and the goodness of his creation.

It follows from unity and goodness that reason and order are proper parts of the creation. St Paul says, as something not to be questioned, that God is a God of order not of confusion, and I think that if you look through the Genesis stories carefully, not only that of Creation in Chapter 1 but those which follow also, you will see an emphasis on order and harmony. The ideal to be sought is one in which all things work together, each performing its own function in a grand design. And if we want to discover what this grand design is we have to pierce through the appearances which surround us and to contemplate the source of our being, God, though in this life we are unlikely to get more than part of the way, to see more than glimpses of the truth. Nevertheless the Biblical view of Creation is opposed to much that is being taught in our modern society, to the nihilism, anarchy, and violence which are being put forward as the answers to our problems. Against those doctrines is asserted the power of reason and intelligence to investigate, to shape, to order, to control. There is a curious little passage in the second chapter of Genesis which describes the first man giving names to all the animals:

> So from the soil God fashioned all the wild beasts and all the birds of heaven. These he brought to the man to see what he would call them; each one was to bear the name the man would give it. The man gave names to all the cattle, all the birds of heaven and all the wild beasts. (Genesis 2:19–20)

The main point of the story as it stands in that chapter is to lead up to the creation of woman, for the man finds no companion in the birds and the beasts, but early Christian commentators rightly saw in the giving of names the exercise of reason to distinguish and to set in order.

This exercise of reason by man leads to the consideration of the place which man occupies in this whole story. In the Babylonian myths the creation of man comes rather as an afterthought to supply a service for the gods. In the Hebrew story the creation of man is the climax, everything leads up to it, and there is a distinct emphasis on the deliberation taken about this by the Creator, signified in the words: 'Let us make man in our own image, in the likeness of ourselves.' These words 'image' and 'likeness'

21

are clearly intended to mark man off from the animals and to indicate a special relationship to God. They have usually been understood to mean the gift of self-conscious reason which distinguishes man from the animals, the power to reflect, to reason, to choose, to pass in thought beyond the limits of the present time and the present world, the ability to reflect on the past and to plan for the future. Hamlet puts it thus:

> What a piece of work is a man! How noble in reason! how infinite in faculty! in form, in moving, how express and admirable! in action how like an angel! in apprehension how like a god! the beauty of the world! the paragon of animals!

And man is set to be master of all living things, to cultivate and to care for the earth. He is to use his reason, his affinity with the Creator, to be a faithful and wise steward of the creation, which means to understand it (natural science) and to use it rightly (moral judgement).

There are some people for whom the sudden vast expansion of our knowledge of the universe, which has come through space research, renders very difficult this traditional belief in man as the head of Creation. The dimensions of thought opened out seem so immense that they find it hard to believe that the human race can have such importance. There has for them been an even greater exaggeration of the difficulties which some Christians felt in the nineteenth century when they found themselves compelled to abandon the chronology of Archbishop Ussher, worked out on the basis of the periods of years specified in the Old Testament, according to which the world was created in 4004 B.C. It must be understood that Christian doctrine is concerned with life as we know it on this planet, and does not have anything to say explicitly about other worlds. I say 'explicitly' because I think it is implicit in our faith that God, being the sole Creator of all things, is known to whatever living creatures there may be throughout the universe in forms appropriate to them. But that having been said, one must observe that so far space exploration has suggested that life is not possible on at least most of the other planets of our solar system, and also that, however many millions of years before 4004 B.C. one is to place the beginning of the world, the fact remains that the actual history of man as we know him is not much more than 4000 years back.

Though we can, as I said earlier, reflect upon the past and plan for the future, and to that extent pass out of the limitations of time, the fact remains that we cannot step outside our human condition and human environment. We cannot be as gods surveying the world as if we were not part of it, or regarding ourselves in the manner of the Babylonian myths as casual by-products of the act of creation. The problem is similar to that of determinism, that if we are not careful we saw off the branch on which we are sitting. If everything is determined there is no point in thought or discussion for they are determined too. If man has no ultimate significance our thoughts are useless and in vain. We come back to the kind of experience with which we started, the fact that we all as part of our condition of life make acts of faith about our condition and its possibilities. But perhaps the immensity of space may remind us of Julian's vision: the littleness of the hazel-nut which is our world – and yet God cares for it.

The Hebrew assertion of man's exalted place in Creation was not made without an element of wonder, as we see in Psalm 8:

What is man that you should spare a thought for him, the son of man that you should care for him? Yet you have made him little less than a god, You have crowned him with glory and splendour, made him lord over the work of your hands, set all things under his feet. (Psalm 8:4–6)

But these same words, just as those of image and likeness, tell us that however close the affinity there is a fundamental distinction between the Creator and the creature. And so, although we speak of God in personal terms and attribute to him qualities which we admire in those around us, we have to bear in mind that we do this only because otherwise we should not be able to say anything at all. God is Creator, we are creatures, and therefore our minds can never wholly comprehend, grasp, or enclose the nature of the Creator. To come anywhere near doing so we must have that complete detachment from the things of this world which alone makes us use them rightly, and it is unlikely that we shall ever in this life find that complete spiritual rest which is in union with God. Julian of Norwich, after the passage which I quoted at the beginning of this chapter, continues by saying:

We have got to realize the littleness of creation and to see it for the nothing that it is before we can love and possess God who is uncreated. This is the reason why we have no ease of heart or soul, for we are seeking our rest in trivial things which cannot satisfy, and not seeking to know God, almighty, all-wise, all-good. He is true rest. It is his will that we should know him, and his pleasure that we should rest in him. Nothing less will satisfy us.[2]

I am aware that in this chapter I have covered a great many things, some of them difficult things, and that many have been touched on only briefly. I have done this deliberately because I made at the beginning the claim that the whole Christian religion rests on the principles expressed in the Genesis story of Creation, and I wanted to give a kind of panoramic view of how this is so. We shall return again and again to most of these points. I once heard Bishop Michael Ramsey say that every point of Christian doctrine contains the whole, and I believe that to be true. For convenience we divide it up, and for the purposes of this book I have chosen certain words by which to do so, but one cannot speak of any part of Christian belief without reference implicit or explicit to the rest. Because the faith is a catholic faith, there is a wholeness, a completeness about it; it hangs together, and it is that coherence which is to my mind one of the most powerful demonstrations of its truth.

II. SIN

I begin this chapter, like the first, with a matter of human experience, but this time with a quotation from a Roman poet, Ovid, two lines which translated run: 'I see and approve better things but follow worse.' This expression, from a very secular context, is paralleled almost word for word by St Paul in the seventh chapter of the Epistle to the Romans: 'I fail to carry out the things I want to do, and I find myself doing the very things I hate.' Here are two witnesses, from widely different sources, to the fact of conscience, to the inner voice which tells us that certain things are right and others wrong, that some things we ought to do and others ought not.

Now it is plain that the dictates of conscience are at least in part influenced by our upbringing, the society in which we live, and by our education. Christian moral theologians have always recognized this. They have spoken of an informed conscience, meaning the conscience of a person who has been brought up in the Christian tradition and who, faced with a moral problem, has sought advice, has studied the relevant moral principles of the Bible and the Church, and has taken his decision after weighing carefully all these things. But Christian theologians have also hankered after the idea that in all men, however uncivilized and ignorant, there are rudimentary principles of morality, and further, that reflection will show that there are certain rules to be observed if human beings are to remain human, rules to which the name 'natural law' has often been given. One of the difficulties of this way of talking has been to get men to agree on what is the content of this 'natural law'. For ancient philosophers such as Aristotle, and for many Christian theologians, the idea of 'natural law' has been greatly influenced by the concept of some destined end for man, a pattern to which he moves, as it can be said that the end of an acorn is to become an oak, and all stages in between are evaluated by their relation to that end.

This view, however, has been dismissed by many modern thinkers as altogether too metaphysical and lacking in rational proof. But in one of the most important of modern books on legal theory, *The Concept of Law*,[1] Professor Hart, formerly Professor of Jurisprudence at Oxford, has argued that we cannot entirely eliminate the idea of natural law. Looking at the matter empirically Hart points out that there appears to be one universal human desire, namely to survive. And he observes that it is not merely that an overwhelming majority of men do wish to live, even at the cost of hideous misery, but that we could not subtract the general will to live and leave intact concepts such as danger and safety, harm and benefit, need and function, disease and cure; for these are ways of simultaneously describing and appraising things by the contribution they make to survival, which is accepted as an aim.

Professor Hart goes on to list five truisms which are at the base of certain requirements common to all legal systems. The first of these is the fact of human vulnerability, which requires rules for the restriction of violence. The second is the fact of the approximate equality of men so that no one man or group of people is capable of continued dominance over the rest, and this requires the making of a system of mutual forbearance and compromise. The third is the fact of limited altruism. People are neither angels nor devils. If they were the first, laws would be unnecessary. If they were the second, laws would be useless. The fact that people are neither angels nor devils but something in between makes a system of mutual forbearance both necessary and possible. The fourth is the fact of limited resources which leads to some minimal form of property and rules for the protection of it. Further, in all but the smallest groups some division of labour becomes necessary and gives rise to laws governing trading, and the observance of promises. The fifth and last is the fact of limited understanding and strength of will, so that sanctions are needed, not as the normal motive for obedience, but as the guarantee that those who would voluntarily obey shall not be sacrificed to those who would not.

These considerations indicate the necessity for a certain rough morality, as David Hume wrote: 'Human nature cannot by any means subsist without the association of individuals, and that association could never have place were not regard paid to the laws of equity and justice.'[2] This can be a merely descriptive account of facts of human existence, but the Christian will see more in it, an expression of the Creator's will for his creatures, and this leads us to the question of how we are to regard the moral law, leaving aside for another chapter the question of how we discover its content.

What we have just been discussing suggests that we ought to regard the moral law as that which is necessary for living a certain kind of life, and not as a code of rules of an arbitrary kind delivered by a legislator, as a headmaster might make a rule that all boys in his school are to have short hair. They are more akin to the principles of hygiene and nourishment which must be observed if one is to have a healthy physical life. In other words, God does not say, 'If you break these laws I shall punish you in certain ways', but rather, 'If you do not observe these laws you will fail to develop in the best way of which you are capable and you are likely to end morally stunted and distorted.' We were made by God, and the purpose of our existence is to know and love him and show that love in our life. The moral law is given to guide us in that; sin is whatever we do other than that.

To sin is to choose some lesser good in preference to God. I call it some lesser good because it is always what a man believes to be good for him. There is generally an impatience about sin, a grasping at some immediate pleasure, a wrong perspective. One aspect of this is the desire for experience, and here we can usefully look at the story of Adam and Eve in Genesis chapters 2 and 3.

In this story man is placed in the Garden of Eden to cultivate it and to take care of it. He is not to be idle but to work, to develop the capacities of the garden and to exercise his faculties. This includes, in principle, the idea of progress. Man has also a moral nature, the power of choice, the capacity to remain innocent. It is more problematical how we should understand the choice which he did make. I will give an interpretation which seems to me to make sense. It is no original thought of mine. I first came across it in a book by Charles Williams, but it goes back in principle to the Fathers and the Schoolmen.

It is of the nature of God to know all possibilities and to determine which should become fact. He can know a thing and its opposite without being affected by either. Evil, as St Augustine says, is the privation of good, and it is part of God's knowledge that he should understand good in its deprivation, i.e. evil, without calling it into being at all. But this is not possible for man. Man cannot know a thing in that way. He knows by experience which affects him. So, in the story, Adam is forbidden to eat of the fruit of the tree of the knowledge of good and evil for 'on the day you eat of it you shall most surely die'. The serpent scorns this warning: 'You will not die! God knows in fact that on the day you eat it your eyes will be opened and you will be like gods knowing good and evil.' Truth and untruth confused. To be as gods meant for Adam to die, for to know evil was for him to know it by experience, 'to experience the opposite of good, that is the deprivation of the good, the slow destruction of the good, and of themselves with the good'.

In the story three consequences follow on man's experience of evil. The first is alienation from God. In the beginning this took the form of a sense of shame. Let me quote Charles Williams here:

> The tale presents the Adam as being naked, and in a state of enjoyment of being naked. It was part of their good; they had delight in their physical natures. There is no suggestion that they had not delight in their sexual natures and relationship. They had about them a free candour, and that candour of joy was a part of their good. They were not ashamed. They then insisted on knowing good as evil; and they did. They knew that candour as undesirable; they experienced shame. The Omnipotence might intelligently know what the deprivation of that candour would be like, and yet not approve it into existence. The divine prerogative could not enter into other beings after that manner; they had to know after their own nature. The thing they had involved confused them, because its nature was confusion. Sex had been good; it became evil. They made themselves aprons. It was exactly what they had determined.[3]

This was the beginning only. It was followed by a darker and more profound alienation, symbolized by the expulsion from the Garden. Sin involves a loss of innocence and the loss of a relationship with God which can never be recovered exactly as it was before. The grim words of Bishop Joseph Butler are all too true: 'Things and actions are what they are, and the consequences of them will be what they will be: why then should we desire to be deceived?'

The second consequence is a change in man's relationship to the rest of Creation. Earth has ceased to be a garden and become a desert, and work has become toil. There is hostility between man and at least part of the animal creation. With the greatest pleasure pain is always to be mingled. Man's alienation from God throws into disorder his whole relationship to that created order of which he was, under God, the steward.

And then thirdly there is a corruption of human relationships. Lust and domination have entered the relationship of the man and his wife, and in the relationship of the brothers, Cain and Abel, jealousy leads to the disavowal of responsibility (Am I my brother's keeper?) and murder. Later, in the story of the tower of Babel, this division is extended to the human race at large, scattered, confused and no longer understanding one another. Again Charles Williams puts it aptly: 'Human relationship has become to a man a source of anger and hate, and the hatred in its turn brings more desolation.'[4]

Three thousand years have not made much difference to the experience of life which these stories reflect, and although they do not provide us with a historical explanation of how this state of things has come to be, they describe something which, so far as we can see, is universal and has prevailed throughout recorded history. They describe something in which the whole human race, past and present (and future) is involved. Even though we do not regard all men as descended from an original pair, or think there was a woman, Eve, who is truly the mother of all who live, yet there is an essential unity of mankind. No man can live wholly to himself and remain fully human. Consider here the contrast between the recluse who shuts himself off from human contacts and becomes turned in on himself, crabbed and hostile, and the Christian anchorite or solitary who, though living with a minimum of normal human contacts, is yet associated in prayer and thought and love with the whole body of Christ's Church.

'Any man's death diminishes me, because I am involved in Mankinde.' These famous words of John Donne are verified countless times when we look around and at our own experience. Modern rapid forms of communication, by drawing us closer together in knowledge of one another, have increased this sense of involvement and responsibility. The concern that we have felt at the Russian invasions of Hungary and Czechoslovakia, at developments in Southern Africa, at natural disasters in various places, are evidence of this sense of involvement. And when we start to think of evil in the world, of the wrong choices that are made, and when we reflect upon our own experience of the influence that others exercise upon us unwittingly and presumably we upon others, it becomes difficult to acquit ourselves not only of concern for, but involvement in and responsibility for, the sins of mankind. What I am trying to say is that sin has not only an individual but also a corporate aspect, and this is expressed in the words of John the Baptist: 'The Lamb of God that takes away the sin of the world', not 'sins' as we are perhaps most familiar with the phrase in the Liturgy, but 'sin', 'the sin of the world'.

This phrase speaks of a deeper stain than the sins of individual men and women. One commentator speaks of it as the lawlessness and rebellion of all created being. Our sense of horror at what happens around us is not limited to the things that men do to one another. Archbishop William Temple tells of an occasion when he was taking some children to the Zoo and met Bishop Gore on the way. When he told the bishop where they were going Gore said: 'Oh, I do hate the Zoo. It makes me an atheist in twenty minutes.' And Temple himself comments that, 'Nature red in tooth and claw' is no fit representative of the God of Love at the infra-human level. The Adam and Eve story speaks sufficiently to our experience to help us to understand how human sin comes into the essentially good Creation about which I was speaking in the first chapter, but the connection between this and the disorder in nature is not so intelligible – though the existence of such a connection is suggested in the story and there is no doubt that in the New Testament redemption is more than once spoken of as applied to the whole Creation.

Bishop Gore's remark raises an age-old problem, one which creates more difficulty of belief than any other. Many books have been written about it, two of the more recent being C. S. Lewis's *The Problem of Pain* and Austin Farrer's *Love Almighty and Ills Unlimited*. For myself, though I find some of these discussions helpful, there is only one convincing comment on the difficulty, and the best expression of it that I know is in a letter written in March 1879 by R. W. Church, at that time Dean of St Paul's, from which I quote two paragraphs.

Church is replying to a letter from a clerical friend putting to him a difficulty raised by a lady of his acquaintance, which was how our Lord could really have sympathized in all human pain, when he could not, by supposition, have known that which gives it its worst sting – its apparent uselessness and helplessness. After saying something directly on this point he continues:

But I suppose that, after all, the real difficulty is not about Him, but ourselves. Why pain at all? I can only say that the very attempt to give an answer, the very thought of an answer *by us* being conceivable, seems to me one which a reasonable being in our circumstances ought not to entertain . . . It seems to me one of those questions which can only be expressed by such a figure as a fly trying to get through a glass window . . . that is, it is almost impossible to express the futility of it. It is obvious that it is part of a wider subject, that it could not be answered *by itself*, that we should need to know a great many other things to have the power of answering. And what is the use of asking what we cannot know? . . . It is one of those questions about our present condition of which, if we choose, we may ask any number, with the same chance of an answer. Why is Nature, being so perfect, yet so imperfect? Why of all the countless faces which I meet as I walk down the Strand, are the enormous majority failures, deflections from the type of beauty *possible* to them? Why are there poisons, and what is the use of poisonous beasts? For a snake, a bee, a wasp, don't want their poisons to take their food. Or to take what to me is as much the crux of our condition as pain – the relation of the sexes, the passion of love; how strange, how extravagant, how irrationally powerful over all the world, how at the root of the best things of life, how at the root of its worst? Strange, ambiguous, perplexing lot for creatures made in the image of God.

Of course this is only Butler again: it is only vagueness and platitude. Every one knows it. But not only cannot I get beyond it, but I cannot imagine any one doing so. And then it comes to the old story: here are facts and phenomena on both sides, some leading to belief, some to unbelief; and we human creatures, with our affections, our hopes and wishes and our wills, stand, as it were, solicited by either set of facts. The facts which witness to the goodness and the love of God are clear and undeniable; they are not got rid of by the presence and certainty of other facts, which seem of an opposite kind; only the co-existence of the two contraries is perplexing. And then comes the question which shall have the decisive governing influence on wills and lives? You must, by the necessity of your existence, trust one set of appearances; which will you trust? Our Lord came among us not to clear up the perplexity, but to show us which side to take.[5]

Jesus Christ came 'to show us which side to take'. That is a large claim and one which will take us into the next chapter on Redemption, but I want to look at it a little further now.

I have spoken earlier about the universal consciousness of sin, and indeed I began this chapter by quoting Ovid and St Paul. Epictetus, the Stoic moralist, asks, 'Is it possible for a man to be faultless?', and answers that it is not. Muhammad in the Koran is ordered to pray for the forgiveness of his sins. Jesus Christ alone among the world's great moralists and religious teachers showed no consciousness of sin whatever. It cannot be said that he taught a low and easy standard of moral living, or that he did not rebuke sin, or that he tolerated it in others. His moral teaching goes right beyond the demands of the law to the hidden motives of the heart. He was stern against the pride of the Pharisees. He taught his disciples to seek forgiveness from God and from their fellows. He told the adulteress to go and sin no more. But he never prayed for forgiveness for himself. Morally he is always the judge. Now this is all very strange, for in our experience the higher a man's character the more he recognizes imperfections in himself, and those men who seem most conscious of their own self-righteousness are usually the most obvious sinners in pride and uncharitableness, hard and repellent. But with Jesus his sinlessness is so much a part of him that his other qualities of gentleness, love, self-sacrifice are illuminated by his innocence. And yet it is not the kind of innocence which is without sympathy and understanding.

On the basis of what we read in the gospels and of the impression which Jesus made on contemporaries, we may well be driven to say, as they were, that Sonship of God by resemblance of character belongs to him in an altogether unique sense. One part of the Christian tradition about Christ's work has been to speak of it as illumination. In him we see what man is capable of being. Even the majority of those who do not acknowledge him as God, or indeed do not believe that God exists, nevertheless venerate and reverence him for his teaching and for the example of his life, in a way that no other great religious teacher has been or is reverenced. Others are looked to for what they have taught rather than for what they were.

Jesus is inseparable from his teaching. It was more than words which made Peter say, 'Leave me Lord, for I am a sinful man'. Face to face with holiness, with perfect goodness, we see ourselves more clearly and we acquire new standards or perspectives by which to see the world around. That is one reason why the contemplation of Jesus has such a central place in the life of the Christian. And this puts us on our guard about the defence of certain lines of conduct on the ground that they are 'natural'. What is generally meant by 'natural' is the corrupted and disordered world in which we find ourselves, and that is not nature in God's design. The life of Christ gives us a different picture of what a man can be, one which might perhaps be called 'supernatural' but certainly not 'unnatural'. It is nature perfected rather than denied.

Christ is so fully and perfectly human that he is able to stand in the same relationship to all men. Although he is firmly in the historical niche of Palestine in the first half of the first century, and, as Paul said of himself, a Hebrew of the Hebrews, he nevertheless belongs to all men in all ages from east to west, from the bickering Christians of first-century Corinth to the Jesus people of our own day, and has been meaningfully portrayed in the colours and features of all races.

Jesus illustrates human nature; he shows sin as a distortion of it, and he also shows the result of sin in his own death. St John writes: 'He was in the world that had its being through him, and the world did not know him. He came to his own domain and his own people did not accept him.' Sin faced with goodness shows its violent and destructive nature. The good is thrust aside, pushed out of the way, killed. In recent years there has been something of a reaction against the realistic representations of the Passion, and against the somewhat morbid dwelling upon the sufferings of Christ which have been a feature of many spiritual writings of the last four or five centuries, but we must not lose sight of the Cross as the rejection of goodness by a sinful race of which we are part. In order to show us goodness Jesus was willing to be pushed out in this way, to be killed, and having been shown this we have to make our own decision, to choose our side. And so I recall Dean Church's letter: 'You must, by the necessity of your existence, trust one set of appearances; which will you trust? Our Lord came among us not to clear up the perplexity, but to show us which side to take.'

III. REDEMPTION

At the end of the last chapter we were talking of Jesus as the perfect man, and of how he illuminates human nature, showing sin as a distortion of it. In looking at him we have a new vision of innocence and goodness, a new world of possibilities is opened to our gaze, a new level of existence set before us. Some Christians have been so greatly impressed by this that they have written of Christ's work in terms of example, and of his death as the death of a martyr, suffering in witness to that in which he believes. On this line of approach man is able to deal with sin because he sees more clearly what is right and is inspired to do it. We may gladly recognize that there are people for whom Jesus is such an example and an inspiration, and whose lives are elevated and enriched thereby, but we must also recognize that for many others example and inspiration are not enough. I recall the two quotations with which I began the last chapter: 'I see and approve better things but follow worse' and 'I fail to carry out the things I want to do, and I find myself doing the very things I hate.' Ovid and Paul combine to testify that knowledge is not enough, and inspiration depends on the degree of imagination and sensitivity in the individual.

Example can be simply another form of law. Paul's constant argument is that law, by showing and commanding what is right, has also the effect of provoking to do wrong. The Ten Commandments may command the assent of the mind but do not necessarily help to strengthen the will. In our condition something more than law and example are needed, something more than knowledge and inspiration. There is one thing which is in the end more powerful than law and that is love. There comes a point at which law gives us up. We have disobeyed it and it turns to punishment, but love never gives up and it exercises a kind of pressure which can, even in human relationships, be all but irresistible. It is difficult to persist in the rejection of love.

When St John starts his account of the last evening of Jesus's life he says: 'He had always loved those who were his in the world, but now he showed how perfect his love was.' There follows the acted parable of Jesus washing his disciples' feet as a token of service, the long discourse expressing and teaching love, the betrayal and Christ's acceptance of death as the consequence of what he is and says and does. 'A man can have no greater love than to lay down his life for his friends.' Here Jesus's work is shown to be something more than the setting of an example, or the illumination of true humanity. There is action in the giving of himself.

But we may still ask what there is which makes this self-sacrifice more than the sacrifice of many others, more, for example, than the sacrifice of that priest who during the war volunteered to take the place of the father of a family as a hostage to be killed. If we ask that question we must look back at three of the things said in the last chapter.

The first of them is the idea of the essential unity of mankind. We are all in this together. I quoted Donne, 'Any man's death diminishes me, because I am involved in Mankinde.' It is somewhat significant that the passage from which that sentence is taken does not appear in the first edition of the Oxford Dictionary of Quotations (May 1941), whereas in the years since then it has become almost the best-known of Donne's writings. Let me give you a little more of it: 'No man is an Iland, intire of itselfe; every man is a piece of the Continent, a part of the maine; if a Clod be washed away by the Sea, Europe is the lesse, as well as if a Promontorie were, as well as if a Manor of thy friends or of thine owne were; any man's death diminishes me, because I am involved in Mankinde; And therefore never send to know for whom the bell tolls; It tolls for thee.'[1] From this came the title for Ernest Hemingway's novel about the Spanish Civil War, *For Whom the Bell Tolls*. In retrospect we can see that that great struggle of the nineteen-thirties was the beginning of a sense of involvement with peoples of other countries simply as human beings, which has grown into the great international movements such as Oxfam and Christian Aid, Voluntary Service Overseas and the many other forms of help for the developing countries. There is now a greater sense of the unity of mankind than at any other period of history, and with it a sense of corporate responsibility.

The second, following on that, is the universality of Jesus. The fact that although he belongs to a moment in history and a particular place in the world, yet peoples of different races and nations have been able to see him in terms of their own physique and culture.

And then there is the third point of the uniqueness of his innocence, the total absence of any consciousness of sin, and the seeming naturalness of this combined with his understanding of and compassion for the sinner.

So with these thoughts in mind, how do we look at the sufferings and the death of Jesus as compared with the death of a martyr? First, that in an altogether unique way we are looking at the murder of the innocent. His complete sinlessness led to his death. Then, that this is not something outside of, external to, ourselves but something in which we are involved. This is what our sins bring about. This is the effect of the sin of the world.

So far horror and guilt, but we see that the love which Jesus expresses will not let us rest there. Two phrases stand out from the pages of the gospels: 'Father, forgive them' and 'I, if I be lifted up will draw all men unto me.' The Cross does not stand over us simply in condemnation but as an invitation, a call. How do we respond to it? Recall for a moment Charles Williams on the Adam and

Eve story. You will remember that he said: 'The thing they had involved confused them, because its nature was confusion. Sex had been good; it became evil. They made themselves aprons. It was exactly what they had determined.' He continues: 'Since then it has often been thought that we might recover the single and simple knowledge of good in that respect by tearing up the aprons. It has never, so far, been found that the return is quite so easy.' Faced by the Cross we find that to make a fresh start hardly seems adequate. Remember the parable of the father who told his two sons to go and work in his vineyard. The first said, 'I will not go', but afterwards changed his mind and went. The other said, 'Certainly sir', but did not go. Our approval is invited for the first rather than for the second, but we might also say that something more was needed than just the change of mind, some kind of apology. So as we look at the Cross we may well feel that more is needed than turning over a new leaf, something which relates to the sin and the spoiling of Creation, something which we might call an apology. But when we reflect that word seems hardly adequate. What is adequate to show our regret for the past, and not only our individual regret but something which will have this corporate aspect and relate to the corporate responsibility which we were thinking about earlier?

When we face ourselves with that kind of question I hope we shall see that there is only one thing that is a really adequate expression of penitence, namely a life lived in perfect and complete accord with God's will. That is something which none of us can show and even if we could, none of us could represent mankind. But the life of Jesus is all that. St Paul writes a sort of hymn in which he says of Jesus that 'he humbled himself, and in obedience accepted even death – death on a cross'. (Philippians 2:8) The death seals the completeness of the obedience. As we have seen, it was the obedience which brought about the death. And then too we have seen that Jesus is

41

recognized as having a representative character so that he can speak and act on behalf of us all. In human relationships people often express their regret by some kind of offering, the making up of some tiff between a boy and his girl-friend, or a husband and wife, is often signified by a bunch of flowers, the end of a quarrel between two business associates by one taking the other out to lunch, a small child will say sorry to its parents by offering one of its sweets. We have nothing that we can collectively offer to God in this way, or indeed individually, but Jesus has made himself our offering with which we associate ourselves. And this offering is properly called a sacrifice, because a sacrifice means something which is made over wholly and entirely to God, made holy.

We tend to think of sacrifice either in terms of the little bits of self-denial that we do from time to time, or in terms of the crude and unpleasant rites that we read of among peoples of earlier and supposedly more superstitious ages. There is a lot about sacrifice in the Old Testament and what is most prominent there is the killing of birds and animals, which is the way of making them over entirely to God. Those sacrifices were attempts to express what men wanted to do and could find no other means of doing, but many of the religious teachers of Israel emphasized over and over again that the only real sacrifice could be one of complete obedience, and that is the main theme of the otherwise rather repellent story of Abraham called upon to sacrifice by killing his only son Isaac. In the story, when Abraham's obedience had been tested to the last point, and only then was he told not to kill his son, we read the prophetic words, 'God himself will provide a lamb,' i.e. an offering, and this takes us to St John in his first Epistle: 'God's love for us was revealed when God sent into the world his only Son so that we could have life through him: this is the love I mean: not our love for God, but God's love for us when he sent his Son to be the sacrifice that takes our sins away.' (1 John 4:9–10)

When therefore we talk about redemption we must understand that there are two aspects to it, an objective and a subjective. The objective aspect is in the perfect life and death of Jesus Christ, who did what none of us could do, and the subjective by which we, looking at what he did, make it our own. Jesus made the one perfect and complete offering of human obedience to God. How we can be involved in this will be material for the next chapter.

There is, however, more that must be said about redemption, for we have spoken hitherto almost entirely about the life and death of Jesus Christ and we must not overlook the fact that all the earliest Christian preaching was preaching of the death and resurrection. For the first Christians the sign that God had, so to speak, set his seal on the work of Christ was that he raised him from the dead.

The resurrection has always been a matter of controversy. The gospels show that it was so, and we remember that as soon as Paul started to speak about the resurrection to the philosophers of Athens some of them burst out laughing. We should not be surprised therefore if something similar happens today. Much has been written about the discrepancies between the different accounts of the resurrection in the gospels, and much ingenuity has been put into harmonizing these accounts; but when we remember that we are dealing with four documents which, in the form in which we have them, were not written until between thirty-five and seventy years after the event, I think that I should regard them with more suspicion if they agreed exactly in every detail. About the central fact of the discovery of the empty tomb they are agreed. Mark stops at that point, though he implies knowledge of subsequent appearances of Jesus. The other three, together with St Paul, have definite accounts of the appearance of Jesus on several occasions, in a form which left no doubt to those who saw him that this was something other than a ghost. Further, all are agreed that there was a definite time when these appearances ended, and the disciples knew that henceforth their relationship with Jesus was to be of a different kind. The evidence is there. One can only get round it by supposing some great conspiracy of deception or corporate hallucination. In the end, however, I think that one will be most influenced by seeing how central the resurrection was to the early Christian preaching, and the effect which belief in it had on the lives of the disciples and has had on Christians through the ages. This makes the resurrection of Jesus something altogether different from the other stories of dead people being restored to life, whether in the Hebrew-Christian context or outside it.

In Christian belief the resurrection is not only the sign of God's approval of what Jesus did, but is also the beginning of new life and an assurance of the victory of good. About the new life I shall speak later: let me now just say a word about victory. We go back to example and inspiration. What are the good of these if death is the end? That is what many have felt and feel, though the stern atheistic moralist will argue otherwise. What has perhaps tortured men more is the triumph of evil in so many cases, and the undeserved miseries of the innocent. We do not have to look further than the Psalms to find the expression of this, or further than our own circle of acquaintances to find examples. If we are given to reading history we can only too often see men borne down by what has been called the tyranny of circumstance. A medieval chronicler wrote of one period through which he had lived as a time 'when God and his angels slept', and there have been many times when men have felt like that, or rather that there is no God, no God who cares. Part of the significance of the resurrection of Jesus is, as it were, to be God's answer to this, the assurance that he does care and that the death of the innocent is not the end. Nor is suffering in all its forms hopeless, but of that again

44

more in another chapter. For the moment let us remember the resurrection as the assurance of the ultimate triumph of good and the guarantee that the moral struggle is worth while.

There is one more thing to be said now about the resurrection. In the second chapter I wrote: 'On the basis of what we read in the gospels and of the impression which Jesus made on contemporaries, we may well be driven to say, as they were, that Sonship of God by resemblance of character belongs to him in an altogether unique sense.' The encounter with Jesus in his life, in his death, and in his resurrection caused the first Christians to do something that was violently against their religious upbringing. They were, we must remember, Jews living under a pagan rule, and not so many years back their fathers had fought a bloody war against the attempt to contaminate their religion by the introduction of pagan cults. A central feature of those cults was the deification of men, which every Jew regarded as blasphemy, an injury to their stern monotheistic belief in Yahweh. And in the first Christian centuries we find this issue lively too among non-Jewish Christians. How many of them suffered for their refusal to worship the deified emperor we shall never know, but there were not a few. All this makes more significant the fact that these early Christians, first the Jews and then the non-Jews, found themselves impelled by their experience of Jesus to speak and think of him as in some sense God, and to use of him language of worship, so that redemption is clearly seen as God's own act. St Paul wrote to the Corinthians: 'It is all God's work. It was God who reconciled us to himself through Christ and gave us the work of handing on this reconciliation. In other words, God in Christ was reconciling the world to himself.' (2 Corinthians 5:18)

IV. CHURCH

Of all our seven square words 'Church' is for many people today the squarest, and yet I suspect that most of those who regard the institution with which we are familiar as futile, irrelevant, or corrupt, would not find it easy to define the Church in terms which to any theologian would be at all acceptable. The reason for this is that the theologian tends to look at things as they are ideally, in this case at what is the essence of the Church, whereas the ordinary non-Christian, and for that matter some Christians, tends to look solely at the institutional appearance of the Church, which changes from generation to generation and usually takes on much of the current forms of society. It therefore always appears to have compromised with the world in ways which those who are critical of the society in which they live find unacceptable.

One of the most astonishing movements of recent years is the Jesus cult, which so far has reached its most general manifestation in the popularity of *Godspell* and *Jesus Christ Superstar*. People have been learning to know the Jesus of the gospels, and learning also to know something of a community of believers, but they do not find it easy to make the connection between the Jesus of the gospels and the Church of today. And yet any serious attention to the Jesus of the gospels must bring us in the end to the Church – not in the form which it took in the time of St Francis, Martin Luther or John Wesley, but in the essential form which derives from Jesus and has continued through all those external changes. We shall try to discover something of that form in this chapter.

In the two previous chapters I have been at pains to emphasize the universality of Jesus, his representative character. Now I must refer to the other side, which I have mentioned in passing only, his setting in the history of a particular people. In the first chapter I pointed out how the Hebrew stories of Creation differed from those of Babylonia, and showed a deeper and more exalted spiritual perception. This is part of what we believe to have been a special calling of the Hebrew people by God. In the Biblical narrative that begins with the call of Abraham who, trusting in God's promises, leaves his homeland and goes out into the desert, not knowing where he is to be led, trusting against all seeming in God's promise that Sarah will bear a son and that from him shall come a people through whom all nations of the world shall receive blessing. Listen to the words from Genesis chapter 12:

Leave your country, your family and your father's house, for the land I will show you. I will make you a great nation; I will bless you and make your name so famous that it will be used as a blessing.

Characteristically, for the Bible is a very realistic book, Abraham is not represented as a model of perfection. He goes out in faith, and on the famous occasion to which I referred earlier, he comes with flying colours through a severe test of faith. On other occasions his trust was not so strong, and like many others since he had to learn the lesson of waiting beyond hope for God to act.

From the twelfth chapter of Genesis onwards there is a community conscious of God's call and promises, and distinctive among ancient peoples by that consciousness. But as in the story of Abraham himself, so in the long series of writings which form Israel's history and our Old Testament there is no attempt at whitewashing. No modern debunking of the people and their leaders is needed, for it is all there. Israel had to learn the hard way, through suffering and defeat and exile, through conquest and oppression by foreign peoples. Some of the Israelites did so learn and left their learning in the prophetic writings, but many others did not, or learned only for a time and then went back to looking at their call as one to privilege rather than to service, and so the picture of the Servant, one of the great images of the Old Testament, becomes that of the one faithful Israelite who for his faithfulness is rejected and killed.

That is the background to the life of Jesus. The people called by God to be the means of his making himself known to all men is reduced in Jesus to the one faithful figure hanging on the Cross. The resurrection shows that to be not only an end but also a new beginning. The old community coming to its end in Jesus gives birth in him to a new. He had gathered round him a band of followers whom, though they did not understand it then, he was training to take up the old mission in a new form; but before they could do this they had to go through the experience of desolation, of seeing their hopes crushed. One of the saddest verses in the Bible is the comment of the two disciples walking to Emmaus after the crucifixion, when they explained to the stranger who joined them the things that had happened in Jerusalem that week, and said, 'Our own hope had been that he would be the one to set Israel free.' (Luke 24:21) That hope had to be purified by suffering and so they had to learn the true meaning of freedom. With the risen Lord's appearance the community was reborn in new understanding and hope and, after his ascension, a new relationship to him.

The nature of this relationship is pictured in a number of images, mostly drawn from the Old Testament but given a new significance. Jesus himself spoke of the vine and of the flock for whom he cares, whom he feeds and guides, and for whom he is ready to give his life. St Paul writes of the relationship of Christians to Christ being as close as that of husband and wife who become, as Genesis had said, one flesh. He also uses the image of the body – Christ the head, Christians the members. St Peter uses the image of the Temple, Christians are living stones making a spiritual house, Christ is the precious corner-stone. I think that the reason why many of these images seem somewhat confused is because the writers are trying to emphasize three distinct things by them. One is the true individuality of Christians and their worth in God's eyes as individuals, the second is the intimacy of their union with Christ so that their spiritual life is utterly dependent on his, and the third is the union that Christians have with one another by virtue of their union with Christ. This then is the essence of the Church – the community of Christians united in Christ.

The first Christians believed that Jesus himself had given certain commands to this community which were integral to its well-being. Two of these concerned religious rites in use by the Jews at that time which were to be used by the followers of Jesus with new meaning. One of them is Baptism. Ritual washings were not unusual in ancient religions, and, as we can see from the gospels, were used in Judaism by religious teachers such as John the Baptist. They seem to have been a sign of penitence and the wish to make a fresh start. Jesus himself insisted on being baptized by John as a sign of his identification with those to whom he was going to minister. Just as simple penitence and turning over a new leaf is not enough without the sacrifice of Christ, so Baptism is given a new meaning by association with his death and resurrection. Paul refers to the way this was understood by the first generation of Christians when he writes to the Romans:

> You have been taught that when we were baptized in Christ Jesus we were baptized in his death; in other words, when we were baptized we went into the tomb with him and joined with him in death, so that as Christ was raised from the dead by the Father's glory, we too

might live a new life. (Romans 6:3–4)

The most obvious symbolism of Baptism is that of drowning. It would be more obvious to us if we were more familiar with Baptism by immersion, which was for long the normal practice and still is in some places. The person who is baptized dies with Christ. A secondary symbol, perhaps more suggested by our practice, is that of washing, making clean, and this too finds its place in the Biblical language. But in the baptismal liturgies it is the thought of water as a source of life which balances water as a cause of death, and this, as I said earlier, takes us back to Genesis. The waters are the first thing out of which all else comes, and running right through the Bible from that first chapter to the last is the theme of the water or river of life.

So then, far from redemption being an escape or deliverance from the material world, we find one of the elements of it used as an instrument in the identification of the individual with Christ. There is a realism about the Biblical language of Baptism which forbids us to treat it just as a sign or symbol, and that is why I have used the word 'instrument'. In Baptism God acts, he does something to us, something happens, something objective on which we can rely, and that is one of the important characteristics about what we call a sacrament. A sacrament is the use of some material object as a means of God's action upon us. God works below the conscious level. We cannot see what he does and we may be unconscious of it at the time, but to sacraments we believe that promises are attached, and by virtue of those promises we can rely on outward signs. This is important because we are creatures of moods and emotions, liable to be downcast or uplifted, affected in our feelings by physical conditions. These signs which we call sacraments are given to us as something firm and sure through all our moods. Baptism is the guarantee that God has given us new life in Christ.

At the very beginning of Genesis we read that 'God's spirit hovered over the water', and in the Creed we confess our faith in the Holy Spirit the life-giver. I shall have more to say about this in a later chapter, but here we must remember that it is the Holy Spirit who comes to us giving life in Baptism. In certain passages of the New Testament the coming of the Holy Spirit is specially associated with a laying-on of hands by the apostles which followed Baptism. In later centuries, when the Baptism of infants had become the most usual practice, this laying-on of hands was separated and reserved to a later date and called Confirmation. It can be thought of as a fresh coming of the Holy Spirit to anoint and dedicate the Christian as he takes upon himself the baptismal promises.

The second rite given by Jesus is what we know as the Eucharist. Again we can see in the gospels how this grew out of familiar religious observances, whether in the form of a fellowship meal or the more specialized Passover commemoration. At the Last Supper Jesus did what no doubt he had done many times before with his disciples. He recited grace over bread and a cup of wine and shared them with the company. The grace in Jewish practice was a thanksgiving to God for his gifts of life and food and the knowledge of himself. Jesus did this at the Last Supper but he associated what he did with what was going to happen to him on the following day. Listen to the oldest surviving account and St Paul's comment on it:

For this is what I received from the Lord, and in turn passed on to you: that on the same night that he was betrayed, the Lord Jesus took some bread, and thanked God for it and broke it, and he said 'This is my body, which is for you; do this as a memorial of me.' In the same way he took the cup after supper and said, 'This cup is the new covenant in my blood. Whenever you drink it, do this as a memorial of me.' Until the Lord comes, therefore, every time you eat this bread and drink this cup, you are proclaiming his death, and so anyone who eats the bread or drinks the cup of the Lord unworthily will be behaving unworthily towards the body and blood of the Lord. (1 Corinthians 11:23–27)

So from an early date Christians met together regularly to 'do this', and there is significance in the day that they chose, for their choice was revolutionary to an extent that familiarity obscures from us.

The six days of Creation were followed by a seventh day of rest, and so in Judaism the sabbath or seventh day was strictly observed. How strictly and how much the subject of legal control we can see from the gospels. We do not know just how soon Christians decided that their day of common worship should be the first and not the seventh day, but the change typified the spirit of the new Church, the beginning of the new creation. The Eucharist is the centre of the building up of the life of the Christian community. We come to it having been already united to Christ by Baptism, and in the celebration Christ's offering of himself and of us in him is brought out of the past into the present, and our life in him is renewed by the sacred meal. Again we have something objective on which we can rely. We do this in obedience to the command of Jesus and we know that his life is renewed in us whatever we may or may not feel. We are drawn away from ourselves, our tempers and our moods, and we learn to rely on him and trust him.

In St John's gospel the place which the others give to the institution of the Eucharist is taken by the account of Jesus washing the disciples' feet.

'Do you understand,' he said, 'what I have done to you? You call me Master and Lord, and rightly; so I am. If I then, the Lord and Master, have washed your feet, you should wash each other's feet. I have given you an example so that you may copy what I have done to you.'

In the Roman Catholic Church this has become a kind of
sacrament and is observed as part of the liturgy for
Maundy Thursday. In the Church of England it survives
in the royal distribution of Maundy Money, at which the
almoner carries a towel in token remembrance of the
origin of the rite. The word 'Maundy' reminds us that we
have here the enactment of the new command of love
which St John tells us Jesus gave in the long discourse
which follows the footwashing. 'Maundy' is the Latin word
mandatum, a command. So in addition to the command to
baptize and the command to 'do this' in the Eucharist,
the Church has the command to love and to show love in
service. I shall have more to say about love in another
chapter. Here I mention it as one of the characteristics of
the ideal or essential Church, and to suggest that one
reason why so many who accept Jesus do not accept the
Church is because the Church so often fails to show love.
I have a great admiration for many of the Victorians and
many of the things that they did, but in the Victorian
Church of England there was an arrogance which I find
it not easy to forgive. A kind of insensitive certainty and
a reliance on position rather than on service made an
unlovely picture of the Church from which we have not
entirely cleared ourselves. And alongside that is the feature
with which we are all only too familiar, the extraordinary
capacity of church people for bickering among themselves,
for putting their own feelings, their own wishes and
possessiveness before the showing of the Gospel and love
of Christ.

The community which Jesus renewed is a structured
community and he gave it the elements of that structure.
He chose certain men as the leaders of it. The gospels are
not as clear as some would like them to be about this.
In places the twelve apostles seem to be the new equivalent

of the twelve patriarchs of Israel and like them to have a unique role. Elsewhere the group of leaders, which may have included others besides the twelve, are given a pastoral charge which goes beyond the life of individuals and requires successors. In Acts and the Epistles we see the first leaders associating others with them, and at the end of the first century it was believed in the Church at Rome that the apostles had made definite provision for other men to succeed to their ministry. In the course of the second century we find that all over the Church this ministry develops into the three orders of bishop, presbyter (or priest) and deacon. The bishop was the father of the community, its president and principal teacher. He alone presided at Baptism and the Eucharist. In the liturgy and the exercise of the Church's care for the weak, the poor and the needy, he had the deacons as what we should call his personal assistants. In the government of the Church the presbyters were his council, but as the Church expanded some of the bishop's sacramental and pastoral functions were shared with them. Thus the life of the community was developed, sustained and directed for the conversion of the world. This pattern of ordained ministry has been retained by most of the Christian Church in the belief that its early and universal development shows the guidance of the Holy Spirit, and that the authority of those ordained comes from the Lord himself.

The Christian life is a disciplined life. Again I shall say more of this later, but now I am speaking of what Jesus gave as marks of his Church. He assumes that his followers will fast, that is, will exercise discipline in relation to their bodies and their spirits. He sets a certain moral standard and part of the commission given to the leaders of the community relates to the maintenance of this standard. It was some time before the Church found the right reconciliation of strictness and love in relation to the moral law, and it has always tended somewhat to fluctuate between the extremes of rigorism and laxity, but without discipline in its life it cannot faithfully reflect the Christian ideal.

Discipline necessarily shares some of the characteristics of law and too much attention to discipline turns men's gaze on to themselves; religion becomes self-centred soul-saving. We so often see in Christian history the desire to domesticate Christ's teaching, to reduce it to what we think we can bring ourselves to observe, or to use it for secular ends of nationalism, commercial prosperity, even of war. The only safeguard the Church can have to avoid these corruptions is to keep its gaze firmly fixed on God, and for this Jesus gave his Church a pattern prayer. He assumes that Christians will pray, as he assumes that they will fast and give alms, but he knows, as the parable of the Pharisee and the Publican shows, that there are prayers and prayers, and so he teaches us how to pray.

Jesus also directed his disciples to heal the sick as part of their proclamation of God's love. Here again is an insistence on the close inter-relationship of the material and the spiritual, of body and soul. The Church has been and still is concerned with the healing of both body and soul. At one time the Church provided the doctors and the hospitals and the nurses. Now that care of the body is mainly provided by other organs of society, but the Church is still concerned with healing and works with members of the medical profession in the healing of the whole person. The use of sacramental ministrations, when a priest anoints the sick with prayer, is one way; but there are many others also, and in a hospital the chaplain is usually one of the most valued members of the staff. Individual Christians, lay or clerical, also may have gifts of healing, and groups of Christians may be called together in special prayer for the sick in body and soul. The ministry of healing has never died out of the Church, but at times it has faded into obscurity. In recent years there has been a remarkable revival and recovery in relation to this ministry, and a beneficial co-operation between the Church and the medical profession.

The danger of doing what I have just done, namely to particularize characteristics of the Church, is that we have a list of items which we tick off as we look at any particular Christian community, and we say, 'Well, the Methodists have got four out of ten, the Roman Catholics have got seven out of ten, the Church of England has got nine out of ten', and so on – and we entirely fail to see the Church as the Body of Christ in which we all participate by our Baptism into him. In other words, faced by the evident facts of disunity around us, we fail to see the real and true whole. The Church seems to be of our making rather than of God's, and the human element, which is ourselves, obscures the divine which alone will make men see that the Church is Christ in the world of today. What I have tried to set out are some of the things which make the glory of the Church, that is the visible manifestation of God's presence, for that is what glory means in the Bible. I have spoken hardly of the Victorian Church. Let me make amends by quoting a Victorian bishop:

> I need hardly say I have never had any harsh feelings towards Nonconformists, and I might add, especially not towards Wesleyans and Primitive Methodists, because I have always felt that it was the want of spiritual life in the Church and brotherly love which led them to separate. The more we can draw near to Christ ourselves and fill ourselves with his Spirit, the greater power we shall have for unity. What we want is more *Christlike Christians.*[1]

To become more Christlike one of the virtues that we need most is humility, which involves a readiness to acknowledge our own inadequacy and a readiness to receive from others. An important part of this humility is the willingness to be patient. From time to time groups of bishops, groups of the clergy, groups of the laity, sometimes a whole diocese or a whole province, wish to press ahead with some major change or reform which seems to them right but does not seem equally right to the greater part of the Church. As many divisions, hardening into lasting schism, have been caused by this as by political and cultural influences. The Church of England, it must always be remembered, although the major church in England, is nevertheless a very small part of the world-wide Church, or indeed of the Church of the western world. The whole Anglican Communion is small compared with others of the world-wide churches. The Anglican bishops form only one part of the much greater world-wide episcopal college which has special responsibility for the maintenance of the faith, and leadership in the mission of the Church. We in England tend to be insular in outlook in religious matters, and we need the humility to recognize our smallness, and how seriously division and disunity imperil both our hold upon the truth already revealed and the Church's ability to discern God's will for the future.

All this should sharpen our sense of urgency in relation to the world-wide Church and make us aware of the need for an agency to serve and maintain that unity. In the history of the Church only the papacy has claimed to be that, but the form in which the claim has been presented has itself been again and again a cause of division. One of the most serious and urgent questions is how the papacy can be reformed to provide that service effectively. Truth and unity are not to be separated. Both are gravely impaired by the divisions in the Church today.

The Prayer Book Catechism describes a sacrament as 'an outward and visible sign of an inward and spiritual grace given unto us'. There are the two great sacraments of Baptism and Holy Communion instituted by the Lord himself as the gospels record, but there are also many other signs of the inward working of the Holy Spirit. Five of these – confirmation, penance, marriage, ordination and the anointing of the sick – have been specially treasured alongside Baptism and Holy Communion. The Church itself might be called a sacrament, for it is a society of ordinary human beings which is created and used by God as a vehicle to bring the knowledge of him and of his love to the world.

A sacrament or a sign of this sort is an assurance to us that God is at work. We cannot always perceive his work. We may on occasion feel nothing, receive no spiritual inspiration when we go to Holy Communion, but because we are doing faithfully what the Lord asked us to do, we trust and believe that through that sacrament our life in him and in his Church is renewed. The Church in its outward manifestation may often disappoint, irritate or anger us, but because it is God's creation we believe that it conveys the message of his love and renews the life of his people; and we can see that through the ages, in spite of many dark days, this has been so. The Church will not always and at every moment be right, but we have the Lord's promise that the truth will not perish out of the Church.

We must be careful not to put wrong limits to our understanding of the Church. Sometimes people identify the Church with the clergy, as when they say of someone who is about to be ordained that he is 'going into the Church'. The bishops and the clergy have their proper place in the structure and leadership of the Church, but the Church is made up of the mass of men and women who are the People of God, and in the end it is acceptance by the whole People of God, bishops, clergy and laity alike, which decides whether or not such and such teachings are an authentic part of the Gospel or a true development of it. The primary calling of a Christian is to live and serve well in the situation and work in which he finds himself. It has been rightly said that a saint is not one who does extraordinary things, but one who does ordinary things extraordinarily well. It is a serious error to suggest, as I am afraid is often done by implication, that every real Christian ought to be doing some sort of 'church work'.

Within the People of God there are special gifts of the Holy Spirit to particular individuals. Thus some have a special gift of teaching, some of prophecy which is to speak with real insight into the present and the future, some have gifts of healing, some of administration, some of entertainment. All these gifts help to develop the health and holiness of Christ's Body, and we should all thank God that they are there. So in the true understanding of authority in the Church it is necessary to recognize that some have authority by virtue of their ordination as bishops or priests and the office which they hold, some by virtue of the special gifts given to them by the Lord, some by virtue of being the ordinary People of God living faithfully the ordinary Christian life. These different sorts of authority have to be related to one another in the right way and each respected by the holders of the others, if the life of the Church is to be balanced and wholesome. But it must always be remembered that the Church is a society for sinners, not a collection of the perfect. There has been in Christian history a recurring tendency to require of those who are to be regarded as Christians perfectness of life, and often perfection narrowly understood, which would exclude from the Christian fellowship the larger number of those who would wish to call themselves Christian but are yet conscious that though they strive after goodness they do not always attain it. Such a tendency has always been exclusive and divisive, and it is difficult to reconcile it with the attitude of Jesus himself, who looked always for the good that was in people and whose love and forgiveness are always available.

The Church is called 'catholic' among other reasons because it is for all men and women, not only of all races but also of all different classes, education, temperament and intelligence, and as the hymn says, we must not make the love of Jesus too narrow by drawing false limits of our own.

V. LIFE

Richard Wagner's music drama of *The Ring of the Nibelungs* is one of the most stupendous works of art ever conceived. Robert Donnington writes of it with some understatement: 'It might, perhaps, not have occurred to anyone but Wagner to start an operatic libretto with the beginning of the world and to end with its destruction.'[1] The whole drama centres upon the gold which in the river bed is just a thing of beauty and pleasure but which, torn from its natural setting, is made into a ring of power by one who renounces love, and becomes the cause of deceit, cruelty, conflict, murder which end only with the destruction of the existing order and the restoration of the gold to its river home. So the great drama begins in the waters and ends in the waters, and perhaps you will recall some of the things I was saying in the last chapter about the symbolism of water in relation to Baptism.

My purpose in speaking of the drama now, however, is to draw attention to the way in which its musical prologue came to be composed. Wagner tells us that in September 1853 he was in a restless mood. After one particularly disturbed night he tried to mend himself by a strenuous and tiring morning walk. After lunch he tried to sleep but instead fell into a strange waking stupor in which he had the sensation of being carried down into deep and swiftly moving waters. 'The rushing of them', he writes, 'presently appeared to me as the musical notes of the E flat major chord, from which arpeggios rose unceasingly, growing into melodic figures in continually increasing movement, yet never departing from the simple triadic tonality of the E flat major chord, which seemed by its persistence to be trying to impress on me that condition into which I had sunk as immeasurably significant. With the feeling that the waves were breaking high over my head, I woke in terror from my near sleep. I realized at once that the orchestral introduction to *Rhinegold*, as I had been carrying it about without being able to find it, had come up inside me. I also knew at once that however things might turn out with me, the flow of life would never pour into me from outside, but only from inside.'[2]

This is a remarkable and nearly unique description of a process of artistic inspiration, of the sense of being moved, possessed by some power inside oneself. Although the Day of Pentecost in Acts is described in terms which suggest the coming of some power from outside – the wind and the flame – the experience of possession by the Spirit is not unlike that inspiration of which Wagner writes. It may remind you of the third of the three ways of approach to God which I mentioned in the first chapter. In all those marks of the Church of which I wrote in chapter four, the first Christians were conscious of God taking possession of them, inspiring them and enabling them to see and do things which had not seemed previously within their vision or possibility.

What we have considered hitherto will lead us to expect that Christian thought about the Spirit will have its anticipations and background in the Old Testament and this is indeed the case. The Spirit there is viewed as operating in various ways. Men are enabled to exercise good government by the Spirit of God within them, to be skilled craftsmen, to preach and to speak of God's will. The Spirit also moves men to behave in ways which are strange and perplexing. The Spirit of God comes upon Saul and causes him to prophesy, which apparently meant that he stripped himself naked or almost naked and uttered strange noises. In the New Testament we find this element also, and quite obviously at Corinth St Paul had to go very carefully because the community there so highly esteemed those who were moved to ecstatic utterances in the Christian assembly. But if you will read carefully through chapters 12, 13 and 14 of his first letter to the Corinthians, you will see how he goes about persuading them that the really important manifestations of the Spirit are in the quality of life shown by Christians. About the same time he wrote to the Galatians that the fruits of the Spirit are 'love, joy, peace, patience, kindness, goodness, trustfulness, gentleness and self-control'. (Galatians 5:22)

In his letter to the Romans Paul particularly links the Spirit with the Christian activity of prayer. The Spirit, he writes, prays in us. All rightly formed prayer must start with the remembrance that we are at every moment of our existence kept in being, sustained, upheld by God, as we saw expressed by Julian of Norwich. We start by consciously resting in God, and we then look to his Spirit within us to guide and lead us in our prayer. Of course much of the time we need the help of things external to us, books of prayers or meditations, the Bible itself, the contemplation of nature and of the goodness of human life, but it is the Spirit within us who leads us to find God through these things and who in course of time may well lead us to find him without them, for we should expect there to be a development, a growth in prayer, in which we come to rely less on external helps and dwell more completely on God himself.

This is one important meaning of the word 'conversion'. To be converted is to be turned, that is turned from looking at oneself to looking at God. In the lives of some people this is marked by the experience of one moment so powerful that it seems to them to overshadow all other development and they give to that moment the name of their 'conversion'. So we speak of the conversion of St Paul, meaning the experience which came to him towards the end of his journey to Damascus, and the conversion of St Augustine, meaning the experience which he had in a garden on the outskirts of Milan on a summer's evening in the year A.D. 386. But for the majority of Christians their conversion is something less dramatic, something which is more of a gradual turning, marked perhaps by moments of decision or illumination. And indeed, in the case of the two whom I have just mentioned, we can see how the dramatic occasion was prepared by previous experiences and encounters, and followed by years of growing in awareness and apprehension.

I do not wish to suggest that conversion happens without conscious choice on our part. The Christian is always in something of a difficulty about how to express his own part in the process for, as we saw in talking about redemption, there is not much that we can do by ourselves. Jesus did something that none of us could do, and we must be careful in what we say that we do not infringe the uniqueness and sufficiency of his work. Paul again helps us with a phrase, when he speaks of himself and his readers as fellow workers with Christ. Without Jesus we could not work; with him and in him we can. Prompted, moved by the Spirit, we take certain decisions, follow a certain course.

There will always be in this two distinguishable elements, one negative and the other positive. Renunciation is a necessary part of the Christian life, and is expressed very simply and clearly in the rite of Baptism where, under the heading The Decision, three questions are put: 'Do you turn to Christ?', 'Do you repent of your sins?', 'Do you renounce evil?' In the passage from the letter to the Galatians from which I quoted the gifts of the Spirit, Paul lists some aspects of evil. He particularizes them as the effects of self-indulgence. 'When self-indulgence is at work,' he writes, 'the results are obvious: fornication, gross indecency and sexual irresponsibility; idolatry and sorcery; feuds and wrangling, jealousy, bad temper and quarrels, disagreements, factions, envy; drunkenness, orgies and similar things.' All this is what the Christian must renounce as a part of his turning to Christ. But there are other things which he may find himself called upon to renounce, wholly or for a time, which are a matter of his individual vocation within the Christian community. 'Marriage is to be honoured by all', says the Epistle to the Hebrews, a phrase picked up by our Prayer Book which speaks of marriage as 'an honourable estate'. But there are those in the Christian community whose vocation involves its renunciation, either as part of a general calling to a different and equally honourable state of life, as is the case with members of religious orders, or because the circumstances of their particular work are incompatible with the responsibilities of a family. Mention of the religious orders reminds us of other forms of renunciation as part of a vocation, renunciation of material possessions, renunciation of certain freedoms.

Besides that renunciation which is essential to a Christian and those renunciations which are part of a special vocation within the Christian community, it has usually been held that there are renunciations which Christians should practise from time to time as part of their spiritual training. I referred earlier to our Lord's assumption that his followers will fast. This book is for reading in Lent, traditionally a period for certain kinds of renunciation. We must spend a little while thinking about this. I have used the word 'training'. In Greek that would be *askesis*, the word from which 'ascetic' and 'asceticism' come. These terms are a commonplace of all religions but we need to think about what is distinctive in the Christian use of them, and it is all the more important to do so because of the attraction that Eastern mysticism in its various forms seems to have for some people in our society today. Asceticism is a part of all mystical training.

In all Asiatic religions there seem to be two principles at work. One, on which the asceticism is based, is a contempt for life and Creation as things from which we must aim to be freed. So the Hindu holy man is marked first of all by his contempt for and repudiation of all worldly goods. He lives entirely on alms, is independent even of clothing, and will not sleep inside a house. The aim is a freeing of self from its surroundings, training the mind to such a state that nothing on earth can distract it, training the body till it becomes insensible to pain. The self-tortures of the Hindu fakir are intended to prove how far he is beyond the reach of suffering, not how much he can endure. The second principle is that through this process of detachment one acquires the knowledge and wisdom of another world and eventually loses oneself in the contemplation of the great Unknown.

Christianity has also its asceticism and mysticism but they are markedly different because they rest on a different basis. As I was at pains to stress in the first chapter, we have no contempt for life and Creation; rather we estimate them highly as the work of God, good things given for man to direct and rule. Our asceticism is a means of getting things in the right order. We have to learn a certain detachment from created things because we know that otherwise they come to dominate instead of to serve. In the cause of a greater good we have to renounce wholly or partially lesser goods which interfere with it. It is a commonplace of experience that in order to do one thing well we have to give up others. There must be a choice of what can be done in limited time. The man who wants to be a singer must not shout himself hoarse at a football match. The athlete must be careful of his diet and physical fitness. Christian asceticism, then, is based on the goodness, not the evil, of creation.

The difference is strikingly exemplified in the Christian attitude to suffering. The Christian neither pretends that it does not exist except in the mind, nor does he train himself like the fakir to go beyond its reach. He endures suffering positively, seeing in it a means of entering into the sufferings of Christ and being in that intimate sense a fellow worker with him. A priest who worked for many years in India writes of a Bengali Christian woman who was grievously, and as it turned out incurably, afflicted with leprosy. She lived in a government institution for lepers, reaching an old age, becoming gradually handless, footless, blind. 'Her happy vocation,' he writes,

> was to tell other patients of the love and goodness of God revealed and imparted in Christ. Her message to them was that this light affliction, light when you think of unending gladness and health, was working for them more and more exceedingly an eternal weight of glory. She lived not a resigned life but a triumphant, radiant life. In his will was not only her peace but her joy . . . Every one who went to see her came away better, and many of her fellow patients through her were brought to our Lord.[3]

Christian mysticism is the result of conscious intercourse in prayer with a personal God and not the loss of one's identity in the contemplation of the great Unknown. There is an ancient saying that the end of man is the vision of God, that is that man is made so that he finds his fulfilment in seeing God. The vision of God is the goal of human life and therefore the determinant of Christian conduct. In the last chapter of his great book on *The Vision of God* Dr K. E. Kirk deals with the suggestion that this is in fact a selfish goal to be contrasted unfavourably with that of service. He is at pains to emphasize that in the best Christian thought the vision is held to be a corporate one, and also that the chief stress must be upon looking *towards* God rather than upon the attainment of some kind of rapture or mystical experience. Let me quote the paragraph which ends that section of his book:

> The doctrine that the 'end of man is the vision of God', as a practical maxim for life, implies that the Christian should set himself first of all to focus his thought upon God in the spirit of worship. It implies this of necessity, and of necessity it implies nothing more – nothing what-

ever as to the achieving of pleasures, rapture, exaltation in the act of worship. The only achievement man has the right to hope for is that of greater Christian saintliness – greater zeal for service – coming from this direction of the heart and mind to God. It can hardly be denied that in so far as unselfishness is possible in this life at all this is an unselfish ideal. To look towards God, and from that 'look' to acquire insight both into the follies of one's own heart and the needs of one's neighbours, with power to correct the one no less than to serve the other – this is something very remote from any quest for 'religious experience' for its own sake. Yet this, and nothing else, is what the vision of God has meant in the fully developed thought of historic Christianity.[4]

You will see, I hope, that the distinctive theme which runs through Christian asceticism and mysticism is that of love – love of God and love of man, so intertwined that they grow together. Love is probably the most misused word today, not only in pop culture where it always has been, but also in much current church teaching. From what we have seen in this chapter we shall I hope understand that there is a discipline about love. It is not a sentimental feeling. It requires both a purification of one's own thoughts and motives and a proper understanding of the true wellbeing of those whom one loves. Some Christian writers have justifiably pointed to a contrast between two of the various Greek words which are translated in English by 'love'.[5] One of these is the word *eros* from which comes the English 'erotic'. It is the most common Greek word for love, and the emphasis in it is on the experience which the individual undergoes. Eros 'puts an end to all self-control, raises all the senses to a pitch of frenzy, bursts all the bounds of manhood humanistically conceived, and transports man above himself'. When it is brought into the sphere of religion the religious experience is often sought in sensual ecstasy. In later Greek thought attempts were made to purify the idea of its sensual element, but even there the seeking for ecstasy, for a kind of experience, remains. The writers of the New Testament chose to use another word, *agape*, which in contemporary use meant the mutual respect and sympathy of equals. Christian *agape* adds to this a sense of unworthiness before God and a realization of his love for us which is shown in his treatment of us as responsible people. Our love for others reflects this if we love rightly, that is, if we respect as individuals those whom we love and do not slip into treating them as things for our own enjoyment.

In Dante's great Vision there are three steps to the gate of purgatory. The first is clear as crystal, the mirror in which a man sees himself as he truly is. The second is cracked and scorched as by fire, the step of penitence which follows after knowledge of the truth. The third is blood red, the step of love on which one treads in the knowledge of forgiveness. By climbing these steps the Christian grows in his love of God, and by seeing his fellows in relation to that love comes to love them with a love of respect and active care for their well-being.

Among human relationships the Bible gives a special place to the union of a man and a woman for life, to the exclusion of all others, which we call marriage. In the Epistle to the Ephesians St Paul uses this relationship as an analogy to help us understand the closeness of the union between Christ and his Church. At the very end of the Bible, in the final vision of the Apocalypse, the holy city in which God's people are gathered is represented as a bride and her union with God as a wedding. The love of husband and wife should be expressed in faithfulness, in respect for one another as persons. Their sexual union is not just a physical thing, not just a means of pleasure, but a sacramental union and giving of each to other so complete that for either to have that union with another person is an act of unfaithfulness and treachery.

Such is marriage as the Bible puts it before us. Throughout this history of the Church, however, account has had to be taken of the fact that some in every age fall short of this ideal and that the sin of one or both partners may virtually destroy the union. Different parts of the Church have developed different ways of dealing with these situations, but all are trying to show Christ's enduring love for all his children and also to maintain his teaching about the true nature of marriage, the love and faithfulness that should be in it.

Marriage has a special place in the scheme of human relationships because it is the normal setting in which children are brought into the world, so that they may live their early and formative years surrounded by love and care, with the stable background of a home. The love of Christ, however, is at work in all human friendships, and in all, marriage as well as others, a special element of this love is purity or chastity, that self-denied, self-restraint which is represented in giving rather than getting.

I called the second step to the gate of purgatory the step of penitence. In all our relationships with God and with one another there must always be penitence. In the second chapter I wrote more fully about the nature of sin, its effect upon Creation and upon our social relationships as well as upon our relationship with God. When Christ's work is applied to us in our baptism we are taken into the community of those who are being made holy and our past sin is forgiven, but we continue to live in a sinful world and to make wrong choices both individually and corporately. Penitence is therefore a continuing need, an essential continuing element in Christian growth. But penitence is not alone. It is met by God's continuing forgiveness, and our knowledge of that increases our love. Jesus gave to his apostles, and through them to their successors, the authority to assure penitents of this forgiveness, to declare it in his name. This the Church does both as part of its regular services and in that special rite which it has developed and which is known sometimes as the sacrament of penance. In this rite a Christian can make his confession to God in the presence of a priest, who can both give him counsel and declare the forgiveness of God and of the Christian community which we damage by our sin. The priest is under a solemn obligation not to reveal to anyone in any way anything that has been said to him in confession.

St John's Gospel (chapter 16) teaches that it is part of the work of the Holy Spirit to expose the true nature of sin. Hence just as the Spirit teaches us to pray and prays in us, so it is the Spirit who shows us the truth about ourselves and moves us to penitence.

The inspiration of the Spirit which moves us in the ways we have been discussing is spoken of in the New Testament as the 'earnest' of that which is to come. The 'earnest' was what we should call the deposit put down as a guarantee of intention to pay the full purchase price, so it signifies the Spirit given to us here and now as the guarantee and foretaste of what we are to have hereafter. This introduces another aspect of the Christian life – that it is a life of expectation. I always think that one of the happiest moments in the Christian year is the period between Good Friday and Easter morning – that day which is properly called Easter Even or Holy Saturday and not, as is becoming common now, Easter Saturday. There is an expectancy about that time, often increased by the atmosphere of early spring. This looking forward to the life which is beyond the limitations of time and space which we know here, is a characteristic of the Eucharistic liturgy. 'The Bread of Eternal Life' is an ancient expression for the Eucharistic bread, and our Prayer Book words of administration say 'preserve thy body and soul unto everlasting life'. The Collect for Easter Even has the beautiful phrase: 'that through the grave, and gate of death, we pass to our joyful resurrection'. The Creed ends with 'the resurrection of the body and the life everlasting'.

Many people have believed in the immortality of the

soul, looking upon man as made of two distinct parts, a spiritual one called the soul, and a material one called the body. Sometimes the soul is regarded as imprisoned in the body. Greek religion in our Lord's time had a phrase which means 'the body a tomb'. Belief in the immortality of the soul is belief that at death the soul is freed from the bondage of the body and continues its existence in another sphere. This is not the same as the Christian belief in the resurrection of the body. Again we go back to Genesis, and you will remember that in the first chapter I drew attention to the word 'psychosomatic' as expressing the modern scientific view of the deep involvement of spirit and matter with each other. We cannot think of those whom we know except in their body, for it is through the acts of that organism – speech, touch, smell, sight – that we know others. The body is a part of our whole personality, and the belief in the resurrection of the body is that in the life which we call eternal life our whole personality will share. Of course we are talking of something that we cannot know from experience. We depend upon what has been revealed in the Scriptures on this subject. There we can see Christ himself, risen from the dead, and recognizable to the disciples as the Jesus whom they had known before the crucifixion. But that of course is the risen Christ appearing to those who are still in this life. St Paul, who writes more about this than anyone else in the New Testament, says that we shall be changed, and he has that wonderful passage about the last trumpet; but I think it is worth pondering on what he has said a little earlier:

Someone may ask, 'How are dead people raised, and what sort of body do they have when they come back?' They are stupid questions. Whatever you sow in the ground has to die before it is given new life and the thing that you sow is not what is going to come; you sow a bare grain, say of wheat or something like that, and then God gives it the sort of body that he has

chosen: each sort of seed gets its own sort of body.
(1 Corinthians 15:35–38)

If we have never seen a field of corn we can have no
conception of what will come up when we sow grain in the
field.

What kind of life is this eternal life, on which we have
entered already by the gift of the Spirit in our baptism and
which we shall enjoy more completely hereafter? It is a
shared life. That the Bible makes quite clear. Shared with
all those others who have this same gift, but above all
shared with God. You will probably have realized that
gradually through these chapters I have been developing
those three ways of approach to God which I outlined in
the first chapter, and showing how these correspond to
three aspects of what we know from experience about him.
The first way, to see the Creator in the creation, reminds
us of our dependence upon God, as children upon their
father. The second way, to see God in human life around
us, finds its highest, indeed its unique expression in Jesus
Christ, friend, brother, saviour. The third way, to look
within ourselves, is to find not only the sustaining power
of the Creator but also the inspiration and leading of the
Spirit.

As we can see from the New Testament writings, the
first Christians came to see in these experiences connection
with things that Jesus had said and drew from them the
terms Father, Son and Spirit to describe them. Through
reflection, spiritual experience, and that controversy which
sharpens thought, they came gradually to the conviction
that these ways or experiences indicate more than just
aspects, more than a monolithic deity who shows himself
in different ways to his creation – that what we know
corresponds to something eternal in God himself. That is
what we call the Trinity, and without some such belief it
is hard to see how there could be any life of love in God
himself. But we do not really approach the Trinity by

thinking of shamrocks or numbers or even the contro-
versial terms of Greek philosophy in which the doctrine
has been framed. There is a living plurality in God which
is wholly love, and it is our destiny to share that life.

I cannot conclude better than with some words from the
end of the modern Dutch Catechism:

When we try to penetrate this revelation prayerfully, we
begin to realize that our whole life is in the hands of
an eternal love. Being brought to the Father by Jesus
and filled with their Holy Spirit, we are perpetually
involved in a mystery of love. Since we are privileged
to be the family of God, the most magnificent glory
is revealed to us . . . the whole of revelation, and in
particular the personal love of Jesus for men in person,
points to the fact that God will not let us dissolve into
an ineffable but impersonal Nirvana. He made man
according to his image so that the personal consciousness which we received from his love should never be
lost, but should continually develop, among our family
today, in the instruction of our children, in our tasks,
in our joy, throughout our suffering and through death
into life.[6]

VI. PRAYER

At various points in the preceding chapters I have touched on the subject of prayer. In this chapter I want to write about it more fully, for prayer is an essential of the Christian life. As one of our hymns says: 'We perish if we cease from prayer.'

It was a sensible man who said to Jesus: 'Lord, teach us to pray.' (Luke 11:1) The reply was the Lord's Prayer, the 'Our Father' which is for us the pattern prayer. It begins by looking towards God in love and praying that his will may be done in all the earth. Then in the second part the prayer speaks to God of ourselves, our needs and fears and our relationships with others. At a very early time the Church added to this a third section which rounds off the prayer by taking us back to our starting point, that is looking towards God as we say 'For yours is the kingdom and the power and the glory for ever. Amen'. We have therefore a movement – to look first towards God, then at the world and ourselves in it, and then back to God in praise and love. That is a sensible movement and a pattern which we can helpfully take, weaving into it our own words.

A word which is sometimes used to describe this 'looking towards God' is 'contemplation'. The experience of many Christians through the ages suggests that there is a fairly usual development in prayer, and when there is a wide experience of this kind we ought to pay attention to it and see whether it can help us.

The development of which I speak begins with what is generally called 'meditation'. One takes a theme. It might be a passage from one of the gospels, a psalm, a hymn, or a passage in some non-Biblical book. One reflects upon it, trying to see what it tells us about God, and how what it says applies to us and to our way of life. Then one tries to turn all this into a prayer, asking God's help to amend our life in accordance with what we have seen in our meditation. There are many books of 'meditations' available and over the centuries various spiritual writers have worked out different schemes or systems of 'meditation'. Some people find these helpful, others do not, and it is important to realize that this kind of prayer does not necessarily involve more than is outlined briefly above. It is important not to force oneself into methods and systems of prayer which are not congenial. As Abbot John Chapman says: 'Pray as you can and don't try to pray as you can't.'

For very many Christians prayer has begun with 'meditation' and they have continued in this way for some time. Some have continued in it all their life, and there is nothing wrong or defective in that. Many, however, find that after a time their pattern of prayer changes. The reflective, reasoning, meditating part gives way more and more to expressions of love for God our Father and for our Lord. Single words such as the name of Jesus, or short phrases, are repeated again and again as a vehicle for prayer. So there may develop a state in which one's whole heart and intellect are concentrated upon God, and if words are used they are used without thinking, merely as a means to hold and occupy the imagination and prevent it from being too much distracted by wandering thoughts. So there is a movement towards greater and greater simplicity, as it has been said: 'All our spiritual life is unified into the one desire of union with God and his will.'

This is what is generally called 'contemplation' but that word can be misleading if it is thought to mean that we are looking at something, as we contemplate a picture. Rather it may be expressed in the metaphor which Abbot Chapman gives: 'I am in our Lord's arms; so close to his Heart that I cannot see his Face.'

I think it important to have outlined, however briefly, this very usual development of prayer because I believe that there are many Christians who after a time find their meditation less and less satisfying and may give up trying to pray because they do not realize that God is leading them to a different kind of prayer. We should expect to grow in prayer as we grow in other ways – in experience and in understanding. For that reason it is helpful to have a more experienced person than oneself as a spiritual adviser or guide. This is a service which members of Religious Communities are particularly well equipped and available to provide. A person is often more helpful than a book, but many people have found *The Spiritual Letters of Dom John Chapman*[1] to be of special help.

Another of Abbot Chapman's maxims is 'The way to pray well is to pray much' or 'the less you pray the worse it goes'. The devotees of Transcendental Meditation, who are to be found in many different walks of life, generally give two periods of twenty minutes each day to meditation. Is it too much to expect the serious Christian to devote at least one period of twenty minutes each day? It is important to have a fixed length of time in which we try to pray. It is the trying, the will to pray, that matters rather than any obvious success as shown by our feelings. The Holy Spirit works in the depth of our being in ways not immediately apparent to us. The fruits of prayer may only be perceived after a long period of time. We pray, or try to pray, in faith; that is, we pray and we leave the outcome in God's hands, trusting that his love and goodness will bring what is best in the circumstances we and others have made.

Something similar must be said about that area of prayer which is called intercession. Here, perhaps even more than in meditation and contemplation, the question arises, 'What are we doing, or what are we trying to do, when we pray for people and for situations? Are we trying to bend God to our desires?' One of the most helpful discussions of this problem that I know is to be found in the last chapter of J. A. Baker's *The Foolishness of God*, the chapter called 'Man in the presence of God'. I will quote three sentences from it:

We are not engaged in creating or producing anything, but in becoming aware of what is already the fact, namely that God is immediately and intimately present both to ourselves and to the ones for whom we are praying. Our task is to hold the awareness of this fact in the still centre of our being, to unite our love for them with God's love, in the quiet but total confidence that he will use our love to help bring about the good in them which we both desire. In technical terms, therefore, intercession is a form of that kind of prayer known as 'contemplation', with the special feature that here we contemplate not God in himself but God in his relationship of love towards those whom we also love; and on the basis of our partnership with him we entrust our love into his hands to be used in harness with his own for their benefit.[2]

We are not trying to impose our will upon God, nor are we trying to move an otherwise indifferent God. We pray on the basis of things that we accept by faith – on the basis of faith in God's goodness, love and goodwill towards all men, and on the basis of faith in God's power, that in the end his will shall be done and that good shall triumph, as the Resurrection of Jesus assures us will be so. We pray also with faith in our freedom, with faith that God has given us free will, the power of choice, and to that extent has limited himself and adjusts the carrying out of his will to our choices. We try in our prayer to bring our will more and more into conformity with his, so that through us his love may have yet freer flow and his will be more nearly done.

Here I find help from another modern theologian, Austin Farrer, who in a sermon on prayer says:

Mind does everywhere flow into mind. How it happens is neither here nor there: it happens. Spiritualism teaches its votaries to make a forced and abnormal use of this power, a use leading to illusion. True religion teaches us the true use of it; and that use is nothing else but intercession. We place our hearts at the disposal of God's will, to spread that influence which he has placed in us in support of our friends' happiness or virtue. We don't have to think a lot of ourselves, or of our spiritual powers, to do that; for influence will flow from us in any case; only, if it is not submitted to God's direction it will be as likely to be bad as good, depressing as uplifting.[3]

In the two passages that I have quoted, prayer for those whom we love and for our friends is explicitly mentioned, but what is said there is applicable to the whole range of intercession, and indeed John Baker later in that chapter says so with some force, reminding us that distance of time and remoteness of contact are of no significance in relation to the immediate presence of God in which we all are. But if our prayer is to be a true expression of love, it is important that it be, as far as we can make it, informed and intelligent prayer, that is, prayer based upon knowledge and understanding.

There is called for from us an effort of imagination. There are human problems which to an extent press in upon us from the newspapers, radio and television, but it is easy to become inured to them. We ought to make time in our prayer to think about them imaginatively, to put ourselves, for example, in the place of those suffering discrimination, to try to understand what it is to be a Jew in Soviet Russia, an Asian in Uganda or South Africa, a coloured immigrant in Britain, or a Catholic or a Protestant in Northern Ireland. Justice and peace must become to us more than abstractions. We must try to see them embodied in our fellow human beings, and feel them as if they were part of our own lives.

Meditation, contemplation, intercession are not in themselves, as forms of prayer, exclusively or specifically Christian. They are found in other religions and some Christians have found that they can learn much about prayer from the holy men of other faiths. These forms of prayer are however given a specifically Christian character by their context, by the faith and the devotional structure in which they are set. Holy Communion, Bible study, the Daily Offices of Morning and Evening Prayer, devotional exercises such as the Stations of the Cross, all have their value and importance. Meditation and contemplation could, and in some cases do, make a person completely absorbed in himself. The Christian spiritual structure of faith and devotion guards against that by relating the whole act to the saving work of Christ who is the Way, the Truth and the Life, and so keeps our direction right.

Penitence, too, is vital, as I have said earlier. Contemplation should lead to and require an ever deeper renunciation of all that comes between God and ourselves. As we draw closer to God we hope to see ourselves and what we are more clearly, to be more deeply penitent, more conscious of forgiveness, more completely committed.

Prayer is not an escape from ordinary life and work. The relationship that should exist is well expressed by Gregory the Great, the Pope who sent Augustine to bring the Gospel to Saxon Britain:

We cannot stay long in contemplation. We can only glance at eternity through a mirror, by stealth and in passing; . . . we have to return to the active life, and occupy ourselves with good works. But good works help us again to rise to contemplation, and to receive nourishment of love from the vision of Truth . . . Then, once more moving back to the life of service, we feed on the memory of the sweetness of God, strengthened by good deeds without, and by holy desires within.[4]

But we must not think of prayer as a kind of solitary withdrawal to be with God alone, for we are at all times in his hands and at all times members of the Body of his Son, the Church. Through our prayer in all its forms, through the sacramental life centred on the Eucharist, through our work and all our activities, we hope to grow in our belief in God's presence and unceasing care, and through that sense of being always in his hands to be more deeply committed in love and service of him, and through him of all his children, our brothers and sisters.

VII. COMMUNION

When I was nine years old my parents sent me away to a small country grammar school in North Lincolnshire. We had no chapel or chaplain of our own and so every Sunday morning the thirty or so of us who were boarders, dressed in Eton suits with stiff white collars, were marched through the streets in a crocodile to the parish church. It was not a very beautiful building, and the pews were the most uncomfortable I have ever met. The service was Mattins, which for the most part we endured with passive acquiescence. There was one occasion when we had a visiting preacher who excited us by a fiery denunciation of the House of Commons for having rejected the Revised Prayer Book in 1928; and on some Sundays the first lesson was read by a local bank manager who had obviously missed his vocation as an actor. I remember an eloquent rendering of David's grief at the death of Absalom. But mostly it was just part of the Sunday routine.

On the first Sunday in the month, however, the service was different. The Vicar appeared in different robes, with two attendants, and instead of Mattins there was a Sung Communion. The whole atmosphere was changed, and the service seemed to come alive. Instead of all the talking which flowed over our heads, there was action and something important seemed to be happening, though quite what it was I think few of us understood. When I was confirmed at the age of fifteen I began to comprehend a little more, and a year after that, when in the course of studying nineteenth-century English history I came across the story of the Oxford Movement, I really saw how the Eucharist is central to the Christian life and that, incidentally, led to my making my first confession, to what some would call 'conversion'.

The Holy Communion, the Eucharist, the Mass or whatever name we call it, sums up the whole central content of the Christian faith. It contains within itself what Christianity is all about, and it does so in a form which can touch people of all kinds because it is essentially a ritual act rather than a set of words. Words are a very imperfect vehicle for conveying the deepest expression of our feelings. In the great crises of life, in joy and in sadness, for many people the act of a hand clasp or an embrace conveys more than any words can do. A child wants to hold its father's or mother's hand rather than to have many words spoken. Often in sickness to hold the sick person's hand gives more comfort, more strength, than speech. So the Holy Communion, by being an act, a ritual or symbolic act, transcends many of the barriers which exist between people. It is possible to know and share in what is happening even though one does not understand the words, as many of us find when we share in Eucharistic worship in foreign countries. For example when I visit friends among the Old Catholics in Holland and take part in the celebration of the Eucharist there, although I do not speak Dutch I know that all of us, Dutch or English, are together obeying the Lord's command and receiving his Body and Blood. So too the Eucharist transcends the barriers of class and of intelligence. It means something to the simplest person and to the most sophisticated. All that fits it to be the central rite of a community which is truly catholic, for all men and women. It has an ability to convey something even to those who are unaware of its full meaning, as it did to me as a boy of nine.

The celebration of the Holy Communion is an act of loyalty, an act of obedience to our Lord Jesus Christ. It is, as nothing else is, the Lord's Service. We 'do this' because on the last night of his earthly life he asked us to, and so week by week on the Lord's Day the Lord's people have gathered and continue to gather for this service.

In some modern contexts ideas of loyalty and obedience seem very old fashioned, and to belong to a structure of society which we no longer accept. Nevertheless they have an essential place in the life of any community, and no one can live a full human life except as part of some community. For the Christian loyalty and obedience are principal elements in the relationship that we have with Jesus, and through him with God our Father and Creator. Through loyalty and obedience we come closest to the perfection and fullness for which God made us; we become most truly human and at the same time sharers of the divine life.

There is also in this loyalty and obedience an important element of self-abandonment. So much of our Christian worship easily tends to rest upon our feelings. If we do not derive any immediate satisfaction from the service, if we find the music uncongenial, the hymns badly sung, the prayers and lessons badly read, or if the whole service somehow seems flat and uninspiring, we are apt to be put off because we are seeking for a satisfaction which we do not find. We are right to be critical of a badly conducted, badly arranged service as an unworthy act of worship, but we ought to consider whether at times we are making our own satisfaction the test of the validity of an act of worship, and that is to be fundamentally self-centred. Similarly we can be self-centred in our prayers if we only pray as long as it is easy to do so, and stop praying when things become difficult. Conversion in the Christian life means that we turn from a self-centred existence to one that is God-centred, and in this process regular faithful attendance at the Eucharist is a powerful influence. We 'do this' as a perfectly objective act of obedience, and 'this' carries us through all moods and changes of feeling. We do it because Jesus said 'Do this', and out of that repeated obedience comes in time a deeper loyalty and love than anything we have known.

The Lord's answer to his Church's act of obedience is to be among us in all his redeeming love and power. Already united to him by our baptism, we are taken into his offering of himself to the Father which I tried to explain in chapter three. He offers us in himself, and he makes his offering our own. 'The centre of the Christian life and worship is the perpetual pleading of the ascended Lord at the Father's throne.'[1] So writes Dr Darwell Stone following St Paul in the Epistle to the Romans, where he says that Jesus not only died for us – 'he rose from the dead, and there at God's right hand he stands and pleads for us' (Romans 8 : 43) – and the writer of the Epistle to the Hebrews who says of Christ our High Priest that 'he is living for ever to intercede for all who come to God through him' (Hebrews 7 : 25). United with our Lord in his Body the Church, we are drawn into that intercession because it has been made possible for us to lay hold on his offering and to make it our own. So Dr Stone writes movingly:

By his own gift we offer Him as a sacrifice to the Father, the sacrifice of the living One who died and is alive for evermore. With Him we are allowed to unite ourselves, and offer ourselves, our souls and bodies, with Him to the Father. And thus taking our part in the great offering, we are enabled to pray for our own needs and the needs of all the Church. Into the great stream of sacrifice we pour the joys and griefs and desires of mankind. There are the sorrows of Christ's people, the troubles and perils of nations, the sorrowful sighing of prisoners, the miseries of widows and orphans and all that are desolate and bereaved, the necessities of strangers and travellers, the helplessness and sadness of the weak and sickly, the weakness of the aged and of children, the trials and aspirations of young men and maidens. With the body of the Lord we offer all that is our own, our praise and thanksgiving, our supplications for ourselves and our intercessions for others, our confessions of sin and our resolutions of amendment.

The Holy Communion is the principal way, following upon our baptism, by which the Holy Spirit applies Christ's redemption to us as a community and individually, and daily renews it in us. In the celebration of the Eucharist it is possible, if we will, for our life and the life of the Christian community to be changed, transformed. But that will only happen if we are willing that it should, and all too often Christian congregations are not really willing that this should happen. So it is specially important that we come to the Eucharist with the right kind of preparation, that is laying ourselves open to God in all humility. The climax of the service is when the bread and wine which the Church has laid upon the altar are given back to us in Communion as the sacramental means through which the life of Christ is renewed in us. The recent Anglican-Roman Catholic Agreed Statement on the Eucharist says: 'The elements are not mere signs; Christ's body and blood become really present and are really given. But they are really present and given in order that, receiving them, believers may be united in communion with Christ the Lord.'[2]

Because we are united with the Lord in Communion we are united with one another, and the Eucharist is a sacrament of fellowship. We care about one another as members of the same family. We care for all Christian people, not just for those of our own congregation or parish; and because we care we mind about the conditions in which they live, if they are unemployed, if their conditions of work are inhuman, if they are treated as things rather than as human beings. So the Eucharist impels us to action to relieve those in need. But beyond that we are impelled to search for the causes of human suffering, the causes of injustice. So the Eucharist becomes and has always been the mainspring of Christian social conscience, impelling some to action in the social services, some to action in politics, some to reflection and teaching. This concern springs from the union we have with one another in the Christian family, but it goes far beyond that to a concern for all people, seeing them all as God's children, our brothers and sisters.

The Eucharist has something more to say to us in the realm of social concern because it is an action in which material things are used. In taking the bread and the wine at the Last Supper Jesus reminded us of the goodness of all that God has made, of those great assertions about Creation which we looked at in the first chapter. The material elements of the wheat and the grape are joined with human work to make bread and wine, and so become symbols of Creation and of human life. Jesus took them, and we take them in his name. We bless God for them and they are given back to us, with Jesus giving himself to us in them. So we are reminded that the setting of human life and what sustains it are God's gifts, for the use of which we are responsible, and human work is a good and honourable thing if in it a right use is made of God's gifts. The Eucharist is the central expression of the sacramental principle that God is to be found in all material things, and unless we realize that truth they will not be rightly used, there will be no right ordering of society, no faithful reflection on earth of the City of God.

The great missionary bishop of Zanzibar, Frank Weston, said to a meeting of Anglicans in 1923: 'The one great thing that England needs to learn is that Christ is found in and amid matter – Spirit through matter – God in flesh, God in the Sacrament.' And he went on: 'If you are prepared to say that you are at perfect liberty to rake in all the money you can get, no matter what the wages are that are paid, no matter what the conditions are under which people work; if you say that you have a right to hold your place while your fellow citizens are living in hovels below the level of the streets, this I say to you, that you do not yet know the Lord Jesus in his Sacrament.'⁸ Social conditions in England have greatly improved since then but Frank Weston's words still apply to many of us in many areas of the land. They remind us that we are stewards of God's world, responsible to him for all that we have and do, and that what should characterize the Christian is the desire to serve Jesus in his brothers and sisters, rather than to set our hearts on material gain.

The celebration of the Eucharist is the meeting place of heaven and earth. The very words of the liturgy remind us of that, of the presence of 'angels and archangels and all the company of heaven'. One approach has always been to see it in terms of the heavenly worship depicted in imagery in the last book of the Bible. There the Lamb stands as the eternal offering, and we are allowed to join with the heavenly company in worship, the curtain being as it were drawn aside in each celebration.

The worshipping company includes all who have gone before us in the life of the Church. Death is a physical separation, painful and sad because for the time being we no longer see, hear or touch those whom we have loved on earth. But we are still one with them in Christ, still united in love, and the Church has always believed that we are united still in the bond of prayer. The celebration of the Eucharist is the centre point of our meeting, and that is why such a celebration is an appropriate part of a Christian funeral.

Among the millions of Christians departed this life are some whose lives were of such outstanding quality that they have left a living memory of holiness or of courage and faithfulness in martyrdom. These are the saints who have their special commemorations throughout the year. Their diversity reminds us that God does not wish our individuality to be stifled but rather that his grace should make perfect the distinct personality that he has given to each of us. The saints are examples of many different types of person made holy, and so are an inspiration to us. But they are more than just examples from the past for they live still in union with Christ and among the worshipping company in the heavenly places.

We hear a good deal in the Church of England about the saints. Many of our cathedrals and parish churches have connections with particular saints, and local festivals are observed. I wonder sometimes, however, whether this partakes rather more of the sort of interest in our past which takes thousands of visitors to historic houses, and rather less of a sense of communion with the saint as a living member of the Body of Christ. Although the situation is far better than it was a century ago, I believe that much needs to be done to recover a full sense of the living fellowship of the saints. This should be part of our full understanding of the Eucharist, because it is there above all that we meet in worship with the saints as with all those other faithful Christians who have gone before us.

There is one saint who has no such historical connection but who stands uniquely in a special category – namely Mary the Mother of Jesus. In their love of the Lord many Christians have understandably included through him love of his Mother, and seen the words addressed from the Cross to St John, 'Son behold your Mother', as addressed to all who are disciples of Jesus. At times in Christian history this devotion has been distorted in ways which seemed to make Mary a mediator between us and Jesus, but such distortion is repudiated by orthodox Christianity and should not be allowed to drive out the good which is a real love for and devotion to the Mother of Jesus. Such a devotion helps to bring warmth and tenderness to our religion. It helps to safeguard faith in Jesus as true God and true Man, and it reminds us that at the heart of our religion it was a woman who on our behalf said 'Yes' to the promise of the birth of Jesus and was the channel through which he came into the world to save and redeem us. So Mary has a proper place in our thoughts at the heart of Christian worship as her Son is present in all his redeeming power, and we join with her and all the company of heaven in reverence and awe.

There is a story of an unlettered lay brother in one of the great monasteries who always had a certain book with him at the Eucharist. One day somebody asked him why he had this book, seeing that he could not read. The lay brother opened the book and showed that it had coloured letters in it, and he said: 'At the beginning of the service I look for a page where the letters are black, and that reminds me of my sins and I am sorry. At the Offertory and the Consecration I look for a page where the letters are red, and that reminds me of the love of Jesus and that he died for me. After Communion I look for a page where the letters are gold, and that makes me think how good God is and of the happiness of being united with Jesus and that I shall be with him for ever and ever.' The black, the red and the gold sum up the central message of the Gospel, and the Eucharist is the daily proclamation of that message.

NOTES

CHAPTER I

1 Julian of Norwich, *Revelations of Divine Love*, trs. C. Wolters, Penguin Books, London, 1966, p. 68
2 op. cit., p. 68

CHAPTER II

1 H. L. A. Hart, *The Concept of Law*, Oxford University Press, 1961, chapter 19
2 David Hume, *Treatise of Human Nature*, Book III, Part II, Fontana, London, 1972
3 Charles Williams, *He Came Down From Heaven*, Faber & Faber, London, 1950, p. 21
4 ibid., p. 23
5 M. C. Church, ed., *Life and Letters of Dean Church*, London, 1894, p. 275f.

CHAPTER III

1 John Donne, ed. Anthony Raspa, *Devotions upon Emergent Occasions*, McGill-Queens University Press, 1976

CHAPTER IV

1 B. W. Randolph, ed., *Spiritual Letters of Edward King*, London, 1910, p. 108

CHAPTER V

1 R. Donnington, *Wagner's 'Ring' and its Symbols*, London, 1963, p. 36
2 ibid., p. 42
3 W. G. H. Holmes, *Memories of the Supernatural in East and West*, London, 1941, p. 106
4 K. E. Kirk, *The Vision of God*, Harper & Row, New York, and Hodder & Stoughton, London, 1931, p. 182
5 cf. *Bible Key Words*, 'Love', by G. Quell and E. Stauffer, A. & C. Black, London, and Harper & Row, New York, 1949, p. 23
6 *A New Catechism. Catholic Faith for Adults*, Herder & Herder, Burns & Oates Ltd, New York and London, 1967

CHAPTER VI

1 *The Spiritual Letters of Dom John Chapman*, ed. Dom Roger Huddleston, Sheed & Ward, London, 1938
2 J. A. Baker, *The Foolishness of God*, Darton, Longman & Todd, London, 1970, and Fount Paperbacks, London, 1979, p. 386
3 A. M. Farrer, *A Celebration of Faith*, Hodder & Stoughton, London, 1970, p. 143f.
4 Quoted by K. E. Kirk, *The Vision of God*, p. 252

CHAPTER VII

1 Darwell Stone, *The Eucharistic Sacrifice*, London, 1920, p. 25f
2 Paragraph 9
3 Report of the Anglo-Catholic Congress, London, 1923, p. 185